House Doctor

QUICK FIXES

House Doctor

Doctor

QUICK FIXES

Ann Maurice

with Fanny Blake

HarperCollinsPublishers

To my dear mother... it's about time

First published in Great Britain in 2001 by
HarperCollinsPublishers
77–85 Fulham Palace Road
London W6 8JB
www.**fire**and**water**.com

Design: Neal Townsend for Essential Books
Editorial: Fiona Screen for Essential Books
Photographs of Ann Maurice: Scott del Amo/Cobra Limited

Crown Decorative Products: 2, 24, 26(middle, bottom), 38(middle), 39
(middle), 54(middle), 55(top left, bottom), 76(top), 92(top), 128, 130(bottom),
131(middle), 141, 142, 144; **Chris Ridley**: 10, 12, 15, 38(bottom), 42-3,
54(top, bottom), 55(top), 56-7, 60-1, 76(middle), 77(top left, middle), 88-9,
93(middle, bottom), 94-5, 106-7, 113(top), 120-1, 124-5, 130(top), 131(top
left), 132-3, 143(top); **Dave Young**: 18-19, 26(top), 30-1, 40-1, 44-7, 58-9,
62-3, 70-3, 82-3, 92(bottom), 93(top), 98-9, 104-5, 108-9, 113(top,
bottom),116-9, 122-3, 130(bottom), 136-7; **Michelle Jones**: 20, 27(top left,
middle), 28-9, 34-5, 39(top, bottom), 48-51, 68-9, 74, 77(top), 80-1, 93 (top
left), 96-7, 138; **Stuart Chorley**: 23, 27(top), 38(top) 39(top left), 55
(middle), 64-7, 92(middle), 113(top left), 143(left); **Andrea Cringean**: 27
(bottom), 76(bottom), 78-9, 102-3, 112(middle), 113(middle),126-7; **Bill
Stephenson**: 32-3, 84-5, 131(top); **Siân Trenberth**: 77(bottom), 86-7,100-1,
112(top), 114-5; **Glyn Slattery** 130(middle), 134-5.

1098765432

Printed and bound in Great Britain by Bath Press Colourbooks

A catalogue record for this book is available from the British Library

ISBN: 0-00-712240-3

CONTENTS

nce again I'd like to say
welcome to the world of
House Doctor.
For those of you who are already
familiar with the principles of
'house doctoring' from my first
book, let me thank you for your
continued interest and support
and say how delighted I am to
present you with a second book.
This new book features case
studies and photographs from
the second and third series, 100
snappy, sure-fire tips to help
prepare your home for the
market, in-depth information on
the use of space and colour in
the home, and a brief visit to my
own home in San Francisco.

10 THINGS
YOU SHOULD ALWAYS DO

NEUTRALISE: Tone down your wall colours and floor colourings to provide a clean, blank canvas. Use stronger colours sparingly as accents to create a pleasing, well-thought-out scheme that runs throughout the house. The goal is to create a look that will appeal to the broadest buying audience.

DEPERSONALISE: Get rid of family photos and children's drawings. Your buyer won't want to be distracted by your life. Let them concentrate on the rooms themselves.

DECLUTTER: Tidy up EVERY room. Pack up and store or get rid of everything that you do not use on a regular basis. If a buyer can't even see a room, he is not going to be able to visualise himself living in it.

CLEAN, clean, and clean again. No one wants to live with another person's dirt, so clean like you've never cleaned before. And don't do it just once and then forget about it. Have a regular cleaning schedule involving all family members.

CHECK YOUR KERB APPEAL: The presentation of the outside of your house is as important as the inside. It should immediately say to buyers, 'I'm a lovely house. Come inside', not, 'I'm not worth bothering with; keep driving.'

SO WHAT'S THE SECRET...?

For those of you not familiar with the term 'house doctoring', a brief explanation is in order. As a professional interior designer and former estate agent in my home state of California, I would frequently be called in to prepare a client's home prior to their putting it up for sale. In America we refer to this process as 'home staging', because what we are actually doing is 'setting a stage' for prospective buyers. Extremely popular in California, home staging was a concept relatively unheard of in the UK until I introduced it on national television six years ago. Today 'house doctoring' is becoming a familiar phrase. I wouldn't be surprised to see it soon finding its way into English language dictionaries.

But what exactly is home staging or house doctoring? Is it a form of interior design? At its simplest, house doctoring is the technique of presenting a home in its best light in order to appeal to the broadest audience base, with the ultimate aim of achieving a quick sale at the highest possible price. It is a marketing tool.

House doctoring is certainly a technique that can be learned, although it does help immensely to have a good design sense or 'eye'. In staging a home, the objective is to eliminate as much of the owner's personality (family photos, knick-knacks and mementoes, highly personalised decorating and/or colour statements) as possible. In fact, when I'm staging a home, I couldn't care less whether the client likes the result or not (as you may have already seen in the series!). When working as an interior designer, however, I do exactly the opposite, as in the end the client needs to love the result and to feel comfortable living with it. After all, it is THEIR home.

Staging is an editing process. Everything personal, unnecessary, or extreme is removed from the home and replaced with things that have a neutral, minimal and harmonious feel to them. Interior design is a supplementing process; its goal is to surround the client with beautiful things that have a personal meaning to them as individuals. Staging is done with no one in particular in mind (or rather, with everyone in particular in mind). Interior design is done with the needs and aesthetics of the individual client in mind.

Interior design is highly dependent on the budgetary limitations of the client, and usually reflects their status and lifestyle. People are willing (and rightfully so) to stretch themselves financially in order to create an environment which they feel reflects their personal taste and meets their individual needs. In a staging project, no matter what the asking price of the home, the object is to spend as little money as possible to get the expected result. I try to use a lot of what the client already owns,

KEEP YOUR PETS UNDER CONTROL. Confine them to a specific area while you are selling your home. Many people find animal presence offensive and the smell off-putting. Why alienate them?

DEFINE EACH ROOM OR AREA. Remember, you're selling a lifestyle so make sure your buyer is clear where he can comfortably entertain, dine, study or play.

DIY NOW. Finish off all those little jobs which can often signal that you may have left other, more important things unattended to as well.

BE SURE THAT YOUR LIGHTING IS SUFFICIENT. If necessary, change bulbs to brighter ones or invest in some new light fittings.

ACCESSORISE. Use mirrors wherever possible to maximise light and space. Dress your rooms with carefully chosen and coordinated accessories. Use colour to tie the room together. And don't forget plants, fresh flowers and pleasing fragrances which appeal to the buyer's senses.

arrange it differently, and spend money only on essentials, most of which the client can take with them when they move. I always reserve the last bit of cash for things like fresh flowers, cheery plants, fluffy new towels, colourful cushions, scented soaps and pot-pourri ... those little extras that cost almost nothing, but give the impression of freshness and attention to detail. The entire environment is 'staged' to give positive subliminal suggestions to prospective buyers, in much the way as in the world of advertising.

Home staging has become mainstream practice in selling American homes. But has this successful 'American' idea really caught on in Great Britain? Has the current property boom finally made the British

public sit up and take notice? Given the continued success of House Doctor (now going into its fourth series), the extreme popularity of the first House Doctor book and the increasing number of enquiries that I receive from viewers, I can say with assurance that house doctoring has definitely made its mark in Britain and is here to stay.

I have to admit that I am somewhat amazed by the success of House Doctor and have given a lot of thought to the possible reasons for its popularity. Here are some observations: first of all, there's the simple curiosity factor. Anything that has to do with looking into a person's home is extremely interesting to others. You may have heard me use the phrase, 'the home is the metaphor of the Self'. What this means, simply put, is that a person's home is truly a reflection of who they are, no getting round it. This, coupled with the fact that the British on the whole have a very 'private' culture (it is not often that they share their homes with outsiders), creates an incredible curiosity or 'snoop factor'. Just take a look at the popularity of the tabloids. In America we have Sunday Open Houses, where the general public is invited to walk freely into homes that are on the market without an appointment, and without the owner being home. Only the estate agent is present. Can you imagine this in Great Britain? The great thing about House Doctor is that it allows prospective buyers to do precisely that, and allows prospective sellers to listen to their not always complimentary comments. This appeals to anyone's voyeuristic tendencies, but more so in a culture that values privacy to such an extent.

Secondly, people have commented on how much they appreciate my frank, 'tell it like it is' style. In reality, I am just saying what most of you are thinking, but could never bring yourselves to actually say because it would be considered extremely impolite by British standards. It was explained to me once by one of the directors of the programme that because I was American, and therefore 'classless', I could get away with it. Whereas if I were a Brit speaking to another British person it would end up being a class issue. I'm not sure that I understand the nuance here, but I'll leave that one for now.

Finally, I would have to say that the British as a culture have what I refer to as an 'edifice' complex, and with good reason. They have the highest percentage of home ownership of any country in Europe. When we consider that your home is possibly the most valuable asset you will ever have, then it follows that any new

10 THINGS
YOU SHOULD NEVER DO

CARPET YOUR BATHROOM.
Bathroom carpets do tend to hold
moisture, often look drab and can
smell. Use a water-resistant floor-
covering instead.

**PAINT THE WALLS IN GARISH
COLOURS.** However much you like
them, your buyer may find them
overwhelming and they often make a
room seem smaller and darker. To
sell your house, paint walls in warm
neutral shades.

**LEAVE OUT THE REMAINS OF
YESTERDAY'S DINNER PARTY.**
Nobody's interested in how good a
cook you are or how many people you
can entertain at once. Do the washing
up the night before and make sure all
scraps of evidence are put away
before the estate agent calls.

**LEAVE THE TV OR BLARING MUSIC
ON.** I sometimes hide the television
altogether by putting it in a cupboard
or behind a screen. Controllable noise
provides an unnecessary distraction
when you want people to concentrate
on the room itself.

**LEAVE BEDS UNMADE OR CLOTHING
STREWN ABOUT.** No one wants to
see your 'dirty laundry'.

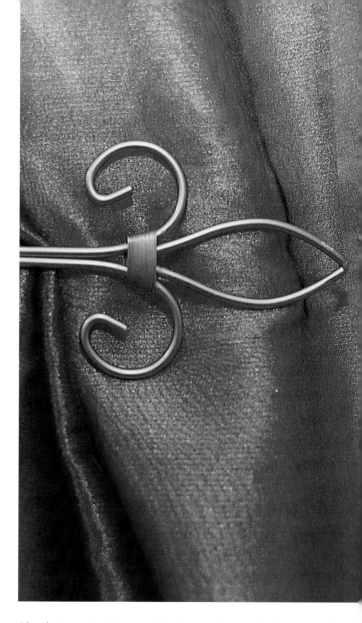

idea that purports to increase its value would generate a huge amount
of interest. The viewing public here is ravenous for any information
having to do with property, DIY, and decorating. What they seem to
especially appreciate about my method is that it has a practical
purpose and, moreover, it can be done on a budget that is within nearly
everyone's reach.

If imitation is the highest form of flattery, then I consider myself truly
flattered. I have noticed recently that there has been a plethora of
new television programmes that seem to have pinched a lot of the
ingredients from Channel 5's *House Doctor* series. I have also noticed
that there is a new wave of House Doctor clones springing up throughout
Great Britain, some unabashedly calling themselves 'house doctors',
others marketing themselves as 'property presentation experts'. Does

this bother me? Not at all. On the contrary, I feel honoured to have contributed to the increased level of awareness in the area of home selling, something that has been long overdue in this country.

Over the past three years, while filming *House Doctor*, I have travelled extensively throughout Britain and have probably seen more of this island than have most natives. As a foreigner who has been able to see first hand how this nation lives, I have come to understand what Winston Churchill meant when he referred to Britain and America as 'two nations separated by a common language'. I also now have a better understanding of the root of the differences between the British and Americans, at least with regard to their homes.

For example, in America we are used to having a lot more space. Therefore, on average our homes are bigger. They are also, overall, built far more recently. Our homes were built with central heating, thus eliminating the need for those horrid radiators you see in every room in British homes, or those boilers displayed on kitchen walls. We have walk-in closets with built-in organisers, rather than a makeshift wardrobe or clothes rail to house an entire wardrobe. We have large-load clothes washers and dryers, and our clothes come out ready to wear rather than damp and creased. We would never think of having a drying rack in the living room, but then again we wouldn't need to. We have garbage disposals and trash compactors and therefore do not need to have a large bin in the centre of the kitchen. Most of our homes were built with electricity, so that unattractive retrofit wiring is unheard of. We have basements and attics and separate TV rooms.

I'm not boasting, just making a comparison. Actually, this realisation has helped me to understand some of the difficulties that arise when applying my principles of house doctoring here in Britain. I have been faced with some real challenges and have tried in each instance to offer a more appropriate alternative.

We Americans like to hide things. We put our TVs and audio equipment behind doors in entertainment centres. Our rubbish bins are under the sink or at the back of our homes. Our washers, dryers, and ironing boards are in the laundry room. How many homes have I seen in Britain where the telly has pride of place in the sitting room? The ironing board is there too. After all, how can you possibly iron without watching telly, and why bother taking it down if you only have to put it back up again? And more astounding to me are the rubbish bins in the front garden as well as prominently displayed in every room of the house.

Finally, this brings me to my number one pet peeve … clutter. You would think that with space at such a premium the logical reaction

THINGS
YOU SHOULD NEVER DO

BELIEVE OTHER PEOPLE WILL WANT TO EMBRACE YOUR WAY OF LIFE. When people look round your house they should be able to imagine themselves living there surrounded by their own things. Don't prevent that happening by leaving your own things, such as photos, travel souvenirs, mementoes, etc. on display.

RAISE RED FLAGS IN THE BUYER'S MIND. Don't leave anything that will make the buyer suspect there may be more trouble and expense than they can see. Does an unattended damp patch signal wet rot? Or a stained ceiling mean that the roof needs to be replaced?

BLOCK THE VIEWS. If your house has splendid views, make the most of them by clearing the clutter from the window ledges, polishing the windows and framing them with curtains.

HAVE THE HOUSE TOO WARM OR TOO COLD. A buyer needs to feel comfortable and relaxed while viewing your home, and not like he can't wait to escape.

ENGAGE IN LENGTHY CONVERSATIONS WITH VIEWERS. Leave that to your estate agent. After all, isn't that why you hired him/her in the first place?

10 THINGS
YOU SHOULD NEVER SAY

'I'VE ALWAYS MEANT TO FINISH THAT.' Implies there may be other jobs around the house that your buyer will have to complete.

'WE'VE HAD A LITTLE PROBLEM WITH THE NEIGHBOURS.' Nobody wants to risk having neighbours from hell. Besides they may get on with them perfectly well. Don't flag up the problem.

'YOU'LL SOON GET USED TO THE NOISE.' Of traffic roaring past on the nearby M1, or from the pub next door? Better try to disguise it, or let your buyers make up their own minds whether or not they can bear to live with it.

'THAT DAMP PATCH HAS BEEN THERE FOR YEARS.' You should have repaired it. What else has been left undone?

'WE WERE TOLD TO REPLACE THE ROOF, BUT WE NEVER THOUGHT IT WAS NECESSARY.' This will be a major expense and inconvenience that no new buyer will want to incur.

would be to eliminate any excess clutter. On the contrary … the British are a nation of clutterholics. We Americans belong to a much more disposable culture. We don't hesitate to toss out something if it is the least bit worn or has outlived its usefulness. In Britain there is a whole culture of wanting to hang on to everything, 'just in case'. Perhaps it is a hark back to the poverty of the war years, or just a reticence to spend money. Whatever the reason may be, the result can be lethal when the time to sell comes.

I do hope that I'm not coming across as being too critical. That's not my intention. I personally believe that people should be left alone to live the way they choose. And what difference does it make anyway if what Jeremy Paxman says in his book, *The English: A Portrait of a People* is correct? 'Unlike some other countries where casual entertaining takes place in the home, the English have a very protective sense of their hearth and prefer the restaurant or the pub.' If you rarely, if ever, invite guests to your home, then there is no real reason to make an effort to change the way you choose to present it … unless, of course, you have put it up for sale. And this is an area where I do have a definite opinion, based on years of direct experience.

So what I have been attempting to accomplish in Britain over the last few years is to educate a nation, not in how to live 'American style', but in how to market their homes 'American style'. The reason this idea has caught on is not that I have done such a good job of selling the concept of house doctoring to the public. It has caught on and is spreading like wildfire throughout the UK simply because it really works. This book is a testimonial to that fact.

I'd like to close by relating a story told to me recently by a young house-hunting couple. After looking for a larger home for quite some time, they had finally found the perfect house. The only problem was that they needed to sell the home they were in before they could buy, and time was running out, as they were expecting a new baby. So they asked the local estate agent to come by for an evaluation. They were given an asking price by this agent, which seemed to be in line with what they were expecting. They then learned that the developer of the new home they had their eyes on would be willing to purchase their existing home in order to effectively complete the sale. The couple discussed the pros and cons of the situation and decided that even though they would most likely be offered a lower price by the developer (who needed to turn the house around for a profit straight away), it would be worth it to secure their deal. They were prepared to accept a maximum of £8,000 less than the estate agent's estimate for the convenience.

In the meantime, the couple (avid *House Doctor* fans) decided to put into practice what they had seen on the programme. They spent the weekend house doctoring and when the developer came around to view their home, he offered them £2,000 more than the estate agent's original evaluation. In effect, they had made themselves £10,000 for a weekend's work. Now YOU decide if it was worth it.

10 THINGS
YOU SHOULD NEVER SAY

'YOU ONLY SMELL THE PIGS WHEN THE WIND'S IN THE WRONG DIRECTION.' And how often is that? Better left unsaid.

'WE'VE KEPT ALL THE ORIGINAL FEATURES INCLUDING THE WIRING.' It will be a massive inconvenience and cost to rewire the building. Modernise it first before you sell.

'WE DON'T BELIEVE IN CENTRAL HEATING.' Make sure your house is warm and welcoming when buyers visit so they don't think heating will be an immediate and essential investment.

'WE FITTED A STATE-OF-THE-ART BURGLAR ALARM. YOU NEED ONE ROUND HERE.' The thought of repeated break-ins will put almost any buyer off.

'WE DON'T BELIEVE THE RUMOURS THAT THIS IS A BIO-HAZARD HOT SPOT.' Do you want to sell your house or not?

HOUSE-DOCTOR STYLE

When I first moved in with my partner Timothy more than ten years ago, it was with the agreement that in exchange for rent, I would be responsible for redoing his house. It was a typical bachelor pad ... horrible kitchen with green formica, very little furniture, posters on the walls, Venetian blinds and a 1970s waterbed suite in the bedroom. Built in the 30s (an older home by Californian standards), in what's known as the 'Marina' district of San Francisco, it is a spacious two-storey condominium with some wonderful original features, none of which had been displayed to their fullest potential. The house itself had loads of character but was absolutely lacking in interior design. As I was just getting my interior design business off the ground, it was a challenging as well as a rather daunting project for me to take on, to say the least.

That was then, this is now and OUR house does not have one room that has remained unchanged. It now exudes what I call 'casual elegance' ... the term that best describes my personal style. The main floor (the living, dining, kitchen and bedroom area) has a comfortable, yet slightly formal feel. Here I've retained an old-world character by using lush, sumptuous fabrics and colours against a subtle neutral background, with antiques, wall glazes and a sophisticated lighting system. Upstairs is a more casual living space that is modern, light and airy. As my house has a roof terrace as well, this is a more relaxed room for indoor–outdoor entertaining, watching television or gazing at the sun rising over San Francisco Bay.

I bought my first home, a 'fixer upper', at the age of 24, and like most young people just starting out, I didn't have a lot of money to spend on 'doing it up'. With my 'good eye', I was forever on the lookout for a bargain. Although I can now afford to go to the designer showrooms for really nice fabrics and soft furnishings, I still find most of the things I really love at charity shops, car boot sales and auctions. I think it is the thrill of the hunt that excites me most. I love combining the old and new or different genres, and making them work as a whole. I've been known to be a bit quirky at times as well.

Having studied decorative painting techniques I am able to see that if something has 'good bones', then no matter what the condition, it can be transformed into a treasure. I feel strongly that original artwork be incorporated into any design scheme, but it does not have to be expensive, just something you love. Timothy and I spent hours combing street fairs, auction houses, galleries, and new artists' exhibitions. Everything on our walls has a history; and many of the ornaments, fabrics and objets d'art are from our various travels.

Our home has been through many different permutations over the years and will, I'm certain, continue to evolve and change as we discover new things and experiment with various styles and decorative techniques. As I always say ... 'The home is the metaphor of the Self.'

SPACE & HOW TO CREATE IT

When selling your home, you must ensure that it looks as inviting and spacious as possible so that it enables buyers to imagine themselves and their belongings already comfortably installed there. There are a number of ways of doing this that will cost you next to nothing, yet will contribute greatly to increasing the value of your home.

DECLUTTER

Begin by taking a good look around your home, starting with the outside. Are there any children's toys, bicycles, skates or shoes on view? How about those soggy old newspapers or piles of post? Overflowing rubbish bins, gardening tools, empty pots or pots filled with plants that have seen better days? If you can answer yes to three or more of these items, then you might have to hire a skip before going any further. If your excuse is that you haven't anywhere to store the items, but that these items are actually useful to you, invest in an inexpensive storage shed for the back of the house.

Now you are ready to step inside. What you will need before you begin is a supply of sturdy storage boxes, bubble wrap or blank newsprint, and some packing tape. Begin by separating all your possessions into four categories: those you absolutely need to have to hand on a daily basis, those you want to take with you to your new home, but really don't have room for or any need to use at the moment, those you are finished with, but could be useful to someone else, and those that are pure rubbish.

Each room's clutter will be slightly different in nature, but with one common denominator; it is interfering with your objective of getting your highest and best price for your home. The entrance tends to be a real dumping ground for hats and coats, umbrellas, shoes and boots, shopping bags, boxes and the post. The sitting room and dining room will usually be cluttered with books, ornaments, CDs, stereo equipment, dead plants, old magazines and even children's toys. In the bedroom, the biggest offender is the wardrobe. Not only could you most likely dump half your clothes without ever missing them (we wear 20% of our clothing

80% of the time), the wardrobe can also be a real catch-all for anything for which you can't find an alternative home ... old luggage, personal mementoes, shoes, etc. The kitchen is another story ... cluttered countertops and cupboards full of mismatched dishes, food that has gone well past its 'sell-by' date, appliances that are never used, empty bottles and cans. Children's rooms are a storehouse for outgrown toys and books as well as clothes, old school projects and collections of all sorts. And lastly, the bathroom ... here the biggest offenders are unused cosmetics and cleaning products, as well as tatty linens.

Subject your entire house to a real blitzkrieg, and then go through a second time with a fine toothcomb. Pack everything you are not

before

keeping into boxes. Get it off the premises NOW. Take some to the dump or the tip, some to the car boot sale or charity shop. What you are planning to keep can go straight into storage in a neat and organised fashion in the cellar, loft or shed. If necessary, temporarily rent a storage locker.

You'll feel better immediately, lighter, as if you can breathe more easily. And you should do – you've just (without it costing an arm and a leg) added value to your home.

STORAGE

Now that you have gone through all your cupboards and created space inside to hold essential belongings, it may still be worth investing in some additional storage items to tidy up your home. Clothes look terrible hung on an open rail so beg, buy or even make a wardrobe in which to keep them. Shoe tidies will keep shoes neatly hidden within your wardrobe. Hooks or racks can often be fitted on the backs of cupboard doors for extra storage, but take care not to overload them. It's better to have your toiletries in a bathroom cabinet rather than on an open shelf, or to buy some pretty storage boxes or baskets. Simple boxes to hold blankets or children's toys can be made from MDF and can double as seats. TVs are better housed in a cabinet — see if you can add doors to an existing shelving unit. If a spare bedroom is doubling as an office, invest in a small sofa bed. Multi-purpose rooms are a terrific use of space as long as they are tidy and well organised.

Look at any dead space you may have and consider whether it could be used for storage. Alcoves are ideal places to put up shelves or a low cupboard. Can you create a cupboard under your stairs or below the eaves? When did you last look behind you as you walked into a room? The space round a doorway can be used for shelving or cupboards provided that they don't block off the passageway. Look round your house and make sure you have allowed enough physical storage space to contain your remaining possessions. How about installing some inexpensive shelving in your cellar or loft for those items you don't use that often?

DEFINE SPACE

Think of the basic needs all of us have in our lives ... sleeping, eating, working, playing, relaxing, cleansing. And then make a point of creating a space for each of them within your home, even if it only takes up a corner. Just rearranging or thinning out the existing furniture in a room can often accomplish this, so that the focus of a particular area, such as the fireplace, becomes clear. I often find proper dining space is sorely neglected in this country. You may enjoy eating off your knees in front of the TV but, when selling your house, you must show the buyer that there is a more civilised alternative. This may mean setting up a part of your living room, kitchen or hall for dining for the purposes of the viewing, but, artfully arranged, it will add pounds to your pocket. Often homeowners have a forgotten or unused space, such as a small closet that could become a study, an abandoned rooftop that could be a lovely outdoor room, or a box room that could make a study, second bedroom or perhaps a kid's playroom. Similarly, the garden, often neglected, especially during the bad weather, needs to be presented as a place for barbecuing, dining or recreation.

DIVIDE SPACE

Sometimes it helps to divide space when attempting to define it. Divisions do not have to be solid or structural but can give the impression of separating one area from another while retaining the sense of space. You might choose to make a curtain or screen that can be easily removed to one side when required. Carefully arranged shelving or stacking cubes are very effective. Garden trellis can be used creatively indoors just as well as out. Anything that you can see through allows the size of the room to remain obvious while the different areas are clearly defined. Furniture placement can force the flow of traffic through the space and can be used to divide a room as well.

COLOUR

Cool colours, lighter values, and plain or minimal patterning cause walls and ceilings to recede and are best for creating a spacious feel. Dark or bright colours, or loudly patterned wallpapers or carpet, make a room claustrophobic. If necessary, call on a few tricks that will enhance the sense of space in any room. If the ceilings are low, paint them almost white (add a touch of yellow, as ceilings tend to grey out in their own shadow) to visually raise them, or use a vertically striped wallpaper on the walls. Avoid horizontal borders or divisions. If ceilings are too high, add a dado rail, or painted wallpaper border to the wall about 2 feet below the ceiling. Paint the ceiling and up to the border the same medium to deep tone. A disproportionately long room can be made to look shorter by painting the two end walls a deeper or warmer colour. Generally speaking, the most spacious-seeming rooms have very little pattern, pale walls and carpet, and use colour as accents in accessories, to prevent the room from looking too impersonal and cool.

LIGHT

It is important that as much natural light as possible reaches the room so make sure the windows are clean and not blocked by curtains or objects positioned in front of them, either indoors or out. Be imaginative with your window dressing. For example, a high pelmet and a wide rail will allow the curtains to be drawn clear of the window. Venetian or roller blinds can be used for privacy or to hide an unpleasant view, but will still admit light. Other window coverings, such as voile or muslin, will allow a diffuse light to enter the room. It may sometimes be appropriate to use spray etch or frosted plastic film to obtain a similar effect. Re-glossing the woodwork in an off-white will help reflect more light into the room. Paints with a slight sheen are more reflective than matt finishes. Light will also be reflected from anything that is made of glass, metallic or crystal, and from smooth or shiny fabrics rather than those that are heavily textured. Reflected light also increases the proportions of a room so work out the optimum position to hang a mirror. Mirrors work well with artificial lighting too. If placed behind candles, above a fireplace, near a pendant light or even lit from behind, they will give the impression of adding more light and space.

Use artificial lighting to highlight various areas of a room to make it appear more spacious. A hidden light source can wash light across an alcove or within a cabinet. Uplighters that throw light towards the ceiling will exaggerate its height, while downlighters will create a warm background light and make the ceiling seem lower. Use light to illuminate any dark corners and unwelcoming hallways and staircases.

FURNITURE

The amount of furniture in a room and its arrangement has a huge effect on the visual space and this needs to be given careful attention when selling. First rule of thumb ... every room must have a focal point. If one doesn't exist architecturally, don't worry, you can create one by the arrangement of furniture. Chairs and sofas should never block the natural traffic flow through the room. Arranging furniture around the perimeter of the room makes the space look smaller and under-utilised. Pay attention to scale and balance. Make sure that the individual pieces are not too large for the room, and that furniture is equally distributed throughout the space. And never, ever obscure an important feature in a room, such as a French window, alcove or fireplace with a piece of furniture; rather, arrange your furniture so that the feature becomes a focal point.

Never has the phrase 'less is more' been more apt than when selling your home. Consider thinning out your furniture and even putting some of it into storage, if necessary.

Creating space is more than just common sense. With a little extra imagination and hard work, you can transform your home into something much more spacious and desirable. All buyers want the most for their money. It's your job as a seller to assist them in realising your home's potential. Don't underestimate the importance of following these guidelines. And remember that by adding space, you are adding value to your property.

ENTRANCES

If your hall is used as a dumping ground for every inanimate object that crosses the threshold – now's the time to clear it. Tripping over bicycles, shoes, umbrellas and schoolbags won't endear your house to any potential buyer.

Never underestimate the importance of properly presenting your hallway. It is the valuable space that sets the tone of your home. It's where potential buyers make the transition from the outside world into your home, often making up their minds about it within minutes of walking through the front door. And so it's vital to make sure those first impressions are the best.

Your hall should appear as light and welcoming as possible. If the walls are painted a strong colour, they will give the illusion of a smaller space. Open it up by painting a fresh neutral colour that leads effortlessly into the rooms beyond. Make sure the doors are painted the same colour as one another and as the frames.

My favourite trick for enlarging a small hallway is to hang a mirror. Every hall should have one. Apart from adding to the impression of light and space, it is perfect for a last-minute appearance check before walking out the door.

Make sure the lighting is as effective as possible. Check all the bulbs have decent shades. A windowless hall will benefit from a halogen light, which gives maximum brightness. Install a dimmer to avoid glare. And if you do have a window, make sure there's one welcoming plant on the sill, not an array of bits and pieces that block out the light and look messy from the outside.

A hall carpet scores high in the wear-and-tear stakes. If yours is particularly shabby, replace it. This might seem like an unnecessary expense but remember, you need to speculate to accumulate. To economise, you could use an offcut or perhaps look at the possibilities of sanding and varnishing your floorboards instead, only using new carpet on the stairs only.

If you can't get rid of ugly features, disguise them instead. A radiator looks far better when it's boxed in and the ledge provides a more useful place for letters than the floor. Your trusty burglar alarm may raise a red flag in the mind of a buyer, prompting him to question whether the house is burgled on a regular basis. Move it to a more discreet position if you possibly can.

Don't crowd your walls with pictures; they will make the walls seem to close in. Hanging one or two carefully will do the trick and provides a welcoming touch.

And don't forget the stairway. Ensure that warm, neutral walls and good lighting issue an invitation upstairs. Check that the carpet is securely fixed and that any handrail is firmly secured to the wall. Remove all personal photos from the walls. Buyers don't need to know your family history – it only distracts them from their view of the house. Make sure the spindles of the banister are all present and correct, and give them a fresh lick of paint to brighten things up.

At last, having guaranteed a great first impression, you're ready to move on to the rest of the house.

TOP 10 TIPS
FOR ENTRANCES

1 Remove all clutter so the passage into the house isn't restricted and the door opens freely.

2 Repaint dark, claustrophobic halls with a warm paler colour to maximise the existing space and light.

3 If the floor covering shows signs of wear, get rid of it. Can you use the floorboards or tiles underneath? If not, recarpet.

4 Be sure that the lighting (both natural and artificial) is sufficiently bright, but not glaring. Update, if necessary.

5 Create a focal point by boxing in a radiator and using the shelf for a couple of favourite ornaments. This will break up the longest hallway.

6 A fresh green plant or vase of flowers strategically placed at your front door adds a bit of life as well as a welcoming touch.

7 Don't crowd the walls with pictures. It'll make them close in. A couple of well-chosen ones is usually enough.

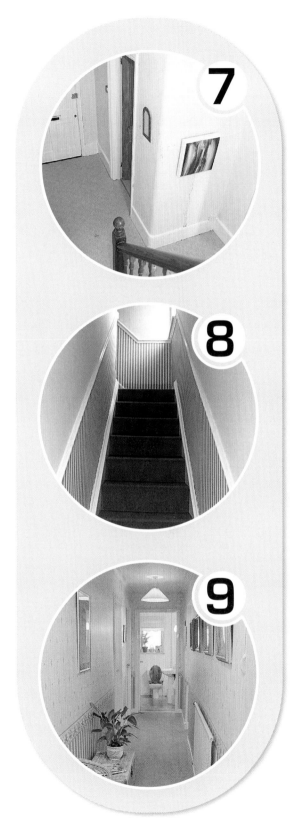

8 The stairs should lead invitingly upstairs, so consider whether it's worth investing in a new stair carpet. Replace missing banisters and, if necessary, smarten them all up with a lick of paint.

9 Open up narrow hallway spaces by maximising both artificial and natural light, and ensuring nothing blocks the route.

10 If you have a burglar alarm, box it in or relocate it, so it's not the first thing anyone notices on entering the house.

ENTRANCE 1 BEFORE & AFTER

Keep CDs off the floor with some of the modern racking that is available nowadays.

Use the space under the stairs for storage without sacrificing space.

Hang a mirror strategically to reflect light up the stairs and into the room.

DIAGNOSIS

Despite a girlfriend moving in, this property had remained very much a bachelor pad. It was horrible. The entrance through a tiny lobby led straight into the living room, where the stairs took up one wall. The turquoise and yellow colour scheme was too strident for most buyers and the worn brown lino needed replacing. Furniture crowded into the room made it seem smaller than it really was and the stairs were hardly an inviting prospect.

DOCTOR'S ORDERS

This may have been the living room rather than the entrance strictly speaking, but there was no getting away from the fact that it was the first space a buyer saw when he came through the front door. So the same rules applied as for all entrances. It had to be depersonalised, neutralised and made to feel as welcoming and spacious as possible.

As in so many of my house calls, the areas that needed most urgent treatment were the walls and floor. The colour scheme was too personal for it to appeal to the majority of buyers so I neutralised it by painting the room a light yellow (Top Tip 2). The tired lino was taken up and replaced with a light wood-effect floor which looked up-to-date and would take the inevitable wear-and-tear of an entrance floor (Top Tip 3). With those two remedies, the room virtually doubled in size. I removed the lamp on the landing and gave a lighter value to the dark stairs by painting the wooden rails ivory creme, removed the dark-blue soiled carpet, and recarpeted the stairway in a lighter colour to make it more inviting (Top Tip 8).

Previously, a grey suite of furniture had been crammed into too small an area and succeeded in making it look even smaller than it was. By rearranging and editing all the furniture and creating a storage area under the stairs, an even greater impression of space and light was achieved. Another favourite trick, which increased the feeling of space, was to hang a large mirror at the bottom of the stairs (Top Tip 9).

When I'd finished, the room had been cured of its case of the blues and looked as if new life had been breathed into it.

A wood-effect floor is hardwearing but also elegant and modern in its appearance.

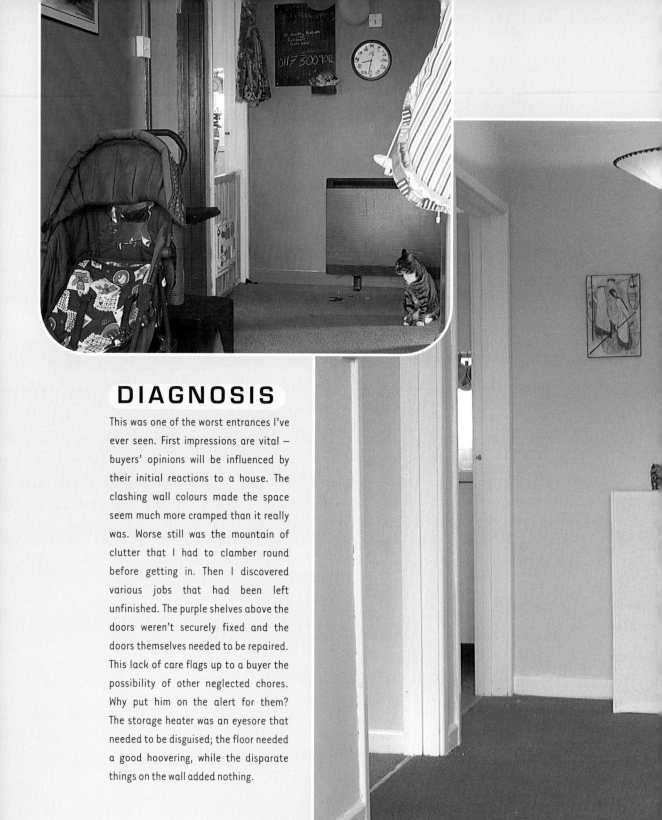

DIAGNOSIS

This was one of the worst entrances I've ever seen. First impressions are vital — buyers' opinions will be influenced by their initial reactions to a house. The clashing wall colours made the space seem much more cramped than it really was. Worse still was the mountain of clutter that I had to clamber round before getting in. Then I discovered various jobs that had been left unfinished. The purple shelves above the doors weren't securely fixed and the doors themselves needed to be repaired. This lack of care flags up to a buyer the possibility of other neglected chores. Why put him on the alert for them? The storage heater was an eyesore that needed to be disguised; the floor needed a good hoovering, while the disparate things on the wall added nothing.

ENTRANCE 2 BEFORE & AFTER

DOCTOR'S ORDERS

The first chore was to remove all the clutter (Top Tip 1). The hall should draw a buyer into the house, inviting them into the rooms beyond. They don't want to trip over evidence of children or pets. Barring the door to the kitchen with a child's safety gate gave a distinctly unwelcoming subliminal message. We also removed all the books from on high and took down the shelves. The room was already looking bigger.

Next on the agenda were the walls, which we painted in a soft neutral colour with white gloss on all the woodwork, including the louvre doors. Apart from making the space look lighter, cleaner and twice the size, this also unified the look (Top Tip 2).

We boxed in the storage heater and, with the help of a plant and a couple of favourite ornaments, created an attractive vignette (Top Tip 5). On the wall above it, I removed the dreary clock, hung a picture and, of course, a mirror to help things seem lighter and airier (Top Tip 9). A good vacuum and this hall welcomed in viewers just as it should.

Clear up any clutter, such as books, papers, bottles, prams or toys, that bars the way into the house.

Soften overwhelming colours with a new coat of paint to give light and space.

Box in an unattractive radiator or storage heater.

CASE STUDY ASHOVER HAY

Roger Windle wanted to move from his childhood home, Rose Cottage, which he'd owned for the last twenty years because his heart was set on building a new home for himself and his soon-to-be wife, Nattaya.

Rose Cottage was the delightful Derbyshire home of Roger Windle and his Thai fiancée, Nattaya. However, despite being in a particularly desirable spot, the property had been on the market for eight months without a bite. Roger was prepared to do anything that would help it sell.

The problems were clear. Generally, we needed to remove the patterned wallpapers and carpet, the clutter and the darkness. I wanted to make the rooms appear much bigger and brighter and to draw attention to the magnificent views. One major red flag for any potential buyer was the damp in the second bedroom. And the fifties retrofit fireplace in the sitting room definitely had to go. Roger set to with an enthusiasm I hadn't bargained for. He completely rebuilt the fireplace to his own design, installing a wood-burning stove, then he was up on the roof, mending the leak before we could say, 'House Doctor.'

Meanwhile, I was smartening up the inside. The busy carpet downstairs was replaced throughout with a beige one, which lent a greater sense of space. In the dining room, we painted the walls to cover a border, which had made the ceiling seem lower. To my horror, the room was hung with animal heads and farm implements, not forgetting the road-kill victim – a fox – sitting on the window ledge and distracting from the view. Too off-putting for the average buyer, they were all removed. We also painted over the busy living room wallpaper to open the room up. The new fireplace was larger than I'd have chosen, but to make the room seem less crowded, we removed some of the existing furniture. Roger used his tiny conservatory as a laundry room, which made the cottage seem more cramped than it really was. I left the door to it open so you could see the view and added a chair so that any buyer could easily envisage

With the walls painted, a new carpet and the wildlife trophies stashed away, the dining room was ready to be shown.

enjoying the sun there. Going upstairs meant being subjected to Roger's photographic collection of girls on bikes – a turn-off for most prospective female buyers. With the walls repainted the same soft shade as the downstairs and the photos removed, the hall and stairs seemed wider. The master bedroom passed muster but the second bedroom smelled damp and was home to Roger's gigantic drum kit, which he'd used in a Status Quo tribute band. It dwarfed the room. But only until I sent it into storage. By retiling the roof, Roger had successfully removed the damp source, so it was safe to repaint the room a soft shade of blue – but only after the walls had been treated with a sealant to stop any sign of the old damp creeping through. A new carpet and some pot-pourri finished things off. At last Roger and Nattaya had a home to present that was comfortable, welcoming and airy. I left confident it would be snapped up soon afterwards.

Roger and Nattaya take a well-deserved break after completing the construction of a new brick fireplace, which included a modern wood-burning stove.

DIAGNOSIS

The owners had lived in this house for twenty years and I'm afraid it showed. The overall impression was of a dark and unfriendly space, with the busy carpet and general clutter making it seem tight and claustrophobic. It would give buyers the impression of being squeezed into the house when they really needed to feel welcomed and drawn towards the other rooms. The hall and stairway needed to feel lighter, more modern and far more appealing.

ENTRANCE 3
BEFORE & AFTER

DOCTOR'S ORDERS

This Victorian hall badly needed to be brought up-to-date. The first thing to do was to remove the clutter so that nothing was obstructing the way through to the heart of the house (Top Tip 1). Then it was a simple matter of replacing the carpet with another in an acceptable neutral shade that was easier on the eye and looked much more contemporary (Top Tip 3). I chose a soft yellow for the walls so that the space looked larger yet offered a sense of warmth and welcome (Top Tip 2). Painting the ceiling white gave an increased feeling of height while the white gloss on the doors and banisters reflected additional light into what was otherwise a rather gloomy passageway.

The walls were overcrowded with pictures so we thinned them out, choosing ones that would add interest without dominating the space or making it close in (Top Tip 7). Too many pictures can be distracting for a buyer. We want them to be focusing on the finer points of the property you are attempting to sell, not undertaking a critique of your taste in art.

The hallway sets the tone for the rest of the home. It is only too easy to put off a potential buyer by making this a difficult or unpleasant space to negotiate. If you take the trouble to present the hall well, buyers will enter the property feeling optimistic about what lies beyond. When I'd finished the work here, the unfriendly atmosphere had gone, and the light, modern look gave a far more positive feel to the hall.

Running the same carpet through the hall and up the stairs can really bring a space together.

Use pale shades to enlarge the space and to give an impression of light and air.

Hang pictures judiciously so that they enhance rather than crowd the space.

KITCHENS

No new buyer wants to sink thousands of pounds into a house immediately after they've bought it. Your kitchen could cost that much to refit, so don't give the impression that's what's needed. There are certain things you can do simply that will make it look modern, clean and inviting.

Think surfaces. Clear the worktops of all but the most essential equipment so there's plenty of space for preparing food. If you've used the tops of the wall units for storage, clear everything off them.

The cheapest way to give a fresh new look to dark or dated wooden units is to paint them white. Gloss or soft sheen emulsion provides a practical, wipeable surface. Sometimes simply changing the handles is enough. If any of the doors or drawers have come adrift, fix them back. If you don't look after something as simple as that, who knows what attention you pay to the rest of the house? Why be the one to put that doubt into a buyer's head?

If the walls have seen better days, repaint them, taking your cue from the tiles, curtains or flooring. Brightly coloured walls won't appeal to every buyer and take attention away from the room itself. If the floor has taken a beating over the years, replace it with a stylish and easy-to-clean covering. When showing the room at night, make sure the work surfaces are lit properly.

Then it's time to obey my first rule of thumb: Clean, clean, and clean again. Your kitchen MUST shine. Any curtains or blinds need to be taken down and washed or cleaned. Remove all signs of animal life. Many buyers will find the idea of animals in the kitchen unhygienic and off-putting.

Once the room is decluttered and spotless, bring in the colour accents. Coordinate a few key accessories: new dish towels, a bowl of apples (they last longer than most other fruit), toaster and kettle. If you've the space, showcase one or two things to create a stylish and welcoming room. And once you've transformed the kitchen into a room that anybody would want as the heart of their home, it's time to move on.

TOP 10 TIPS FOR THE KITCHEN

1 Clean everything thoroughly. It's essential that your kitchen looks as hygienic and functional as possible.

2 Clear all inessential clutter, including last night's washing up and what's collected on the top of the units.

3 Make sure the room is as light and bright as possible. That means neutral-coloured walls with accents of colour in the room.

4 If the units look dated, consider painting them or even replacing the doors or handles altogether.

5 Check the floor. It should be spotless. If it is worn, replace it.

6 Only have new, neatly folded drying-up cloths – NOT the ones you've been drying your hands on all week!

7 If taps, cooker or hob have seen better days, replacing them is not that expensive and can give a new look to an old kitchen.

8 Finish off all minor repairs. Don't give the impression that an inexpensive new kitchen might be needed soon.

9 Get rid of any evidence of where your pets eat or sleep. Some buyers might find it unhygienic or positively offensive.

10 Baking bread, a cinnamon stick boiling on the cooker, or fresh coffee brewing adds an aroma that appeals subliminally to the buyer's senses. It gives one that feeling of 'home'.

KITCHEN 1 BEFORE & AFTER

If there are any jobs left unfinished, now's the moment to attend to them.

Frame a hatch with pictures in order to make it into a more attractive feature.

Buying new furniture is often a sound investment if it transforms the look of a room.

DIAGNOSIS

I didn't feel the owners had done this kitchen justice. It was a big, bright room but various DIY jobs had been left unfinished: the so-called 'hatch' was just a hole in the wall; the walls weren't completely plastered; the shelves were left unsealed. The furniture was heavy, dark, and badly positioned, making the room seem much smaller than it was. Although I prefer neutral background colours overall, I felt this was just too bland here and the room suffered.

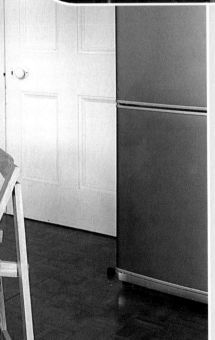

DOCTOR'S ORDERS

It's completely unnecessary to leave those little DIY jobs undone (Top Tip 8). It gives the impression that the house hasn't been cared for and the buyer's mind is immediately directed towards the extra money and time he'll have to lay out to fix them. In this case, we finished off plastering the walls and took the opportunity to repaint them. The tiles dictated a cheery yellow, which suited the size and atmosphere of the room. I decided to make a feature of the hatch by finishing it off properly and then framing it with three pictures.

The furniture was an odd mismatch of church and farmhouse. I felt that the room merited something more contemporary, so persuaded the owners to put the old pieces in storage and to splash out on a brand new table and chairs. It was money well spent because they entirely changed the feel of the room and, of course, they would go with the owners to their new home when they eventually moved.

It's just as important to accessorise a kitchen as it is any other room. In the work area, I used blue accents, which looked great against the yellow background (Top Tip 3). When it came to the table, I wanted something a little different. That patterned tablecloth had to go. It looked old-fashioned and unattractive. Because the table was new, we didn't need to hide the top under a cloth but I felt a runner would give focus to that side of the room. I used a self-coloured piece of fabric, taking the colour from the pictures. The peace lily in a coordinating vase was the final touch.

Focus interest on your table by adding a runner and a potted plant, or a vase of fresh flowers.

DIAGNOSIS

This kitchen was in a tiny split-level flat where space was at a premium. One of the problems was that it opened on to the living area which meant that anyone coming in was immediately confronted by it. The deep blue of the walls gave the area a claustrophobic feel. Surfaces were jammed with clutter and the tiles at the edge of the work surface were very chipped and cracked. I don't think I need to elaborate on the grime and general sense of neglect. A bag of rubbish was left in full view near a miserable-looking old dishcloth hanging from a unit door. Leaving things like that out gives a dismal impression. The most off-putting feature was the ladder leading up to the gallery space above the kitchen, which we replaced with folding steps. Not many buyers would have risked their neck getting up there. Apart from that, this was a question of getting the owner to clean up his act if he wanted to make a sale.

KITCHEN 2 BEFORE & AFTER

DOCTOR'S ORDERS

This had been a bachelor pad for far too long, and it showed. There is nothing more off-putting to a potential buyer than an unhygienic-looking kitchen. Buyers should immediately be able to envisage themselves spending time in there and enjoying food prepared there. Our first job was to clean the area until it was absolutely spotless and replace all the broken tiles (Top Tip 1). Then we decluttered the surfaces of as much as possible, given the general lack of space in the flat (Top Tip 2).

The living area walls had been repainted a warm peach and I felt that a gentle green on the kitchen walls complemented it better than the blue and made the space less claustrophobic (Top Tip 3).

As for those death-trap steps: First we checked whether we had to conform to building regulations, then simply installed a retractable steel spring-loaded ladder, which was much safer.

If dish towels must be in sight, then make sure they are clean, preferably new, ironed and NOT draped over the units (Top Tip 6). As for rubbish — please throw it out.

Reduce surface clutter and thoroughly clean all work surfaces.

Replace all used tea towels with neatly ironed ones that are hung up properly.

If anything looks dangerous, replace, repair, or get rid of it.

KITCHEN 3 BEFORE & AFTER

Dark wood can be overwhelming and will not show off the space you have to best effect.

New furniture can transform the entire appearance of a room, making it a pleasing place to be.

Floorboards provide a warm, country feel, as well as being a practical solution.

Check all the major surfaces and be sure to replace them where necessary.

DIAGNOSIS

This house had a bad case of the three Ds — dark, dingy and dirty. With its dark wood units, blood red walls and green carpet, the kitchen was no exception. The dark table and mismatched chairs didn't do the room any favours either. Things weren't helped by the unit door over the oven, which had been charred by a grease fire. Apart from a thorough clean, the room really needed a good facelift to show it off in character with the rest of the converted chapel.

DOCTOR'S ORDERS

Always look at the major surfaces in a room and check how they can be changed if necessary. Carpet is never a good choice for a kitchen. It soon gets worn and is extremely difficult to keep clean. In this instance we dumped the old one in favour of a new wood-effect floor which immediately gave the room a cleaner, more contemporary feel (Top Tip 5).

It's always surprising the difference a coat or two of paint can make. The walls, which reminded me of a Mexican restaurant rather than an English country kitchen, looked much better painted a muted green. Dated wood units were given a new lease of life in cream and the melamine worktops were revived with a complementary shade of specialised paint (Top Tip 4).

I do try not to replace any expensive kitchen fittings. It's usually enough to improve their surroundings. However, in this case I had to insist that the owners buy a new oven. The old one was in such a bad state that it implied the possibility of having to entirely refit the kitchen — an additional expense that no new homeowner wants to incur (Top Tip 7). They were also persuaded to invest in a new table with matching chairs, which again added to the lighter, more modern country look.

We didn't have to do too much clutter-clearing here, but I felt that the microwave was better placed on the counter by the oven than on the window ledge, where it blocked the light. The finishing touch to the kitchen was a bowl of fresh fruit in the centre of the table (Top Tip 10). What could be more inviting?

CASE STUDY WORCESTER

Sabrina and Peter Squires wanted to move to Europe but not until they could find a buyer for their period cottage

Californian Sabrina Squires and her husband Peter wanted to move to Europe. But they had encountered a problem in selling their 350-year-old cottage just outside Worcester. Situated in between the rolling Malvern Hills and the Cotswolds, it commanded magnificent views, as well as being conveniently near the M5. The three-bedroomed cottage was competitively priced at £299,000, but it had been on the market for a year. Both Sabrina and Peter were baffled as to why their idyllic country cottage hadn't been immediately snapped up and they welcomed me with the proviso that Sabrina wouldn't be doing anything that would damage her long nails.

But it didn't take long for me to see what was wrong. I was practically speechless when I saw the living room which, like the rest of the house, was packed with clutter — Hollywood met olde England head-on. This was definitely a case of too much of a good thing. Anybody looking round was blinded to the

intrinsic value of the property. Unlike the cottage, the two-bedroomed annexe was under-decorated, as well as cold and unwelcoming. At first, Sabrina was resistant to my suggestions but eventually understood that any potential buyer had to be able to envisage moving into their home. To make this happen, we would have to depersonalise the cottage, redistribute some of their belongings and balance the crowded living spaces and the empty annexe. Professional packers were brought in to remove the pieces that Sabrina wanted to keep for her new home, while she held a garage sale for the rest.

Without the clutter, you could see the size of the living room with the emphasis on the stunning view and the original beams. Now we could relocate various pieces and display them properly. Peter had decorated the breakfast room and Sabrina had contributed by cluttering it. Doctor's orders meant we painted over the patterns and cleared the room, defining its purpose. By

From cold and unfriendly to warm and lived-in.

Simple wooden furniture was ideal for a charming nursery.

turning on the heating and making the room look as if it was used, it became inviting. But it was upstairs where I met real problems. The third bedroom had been used as a walk-in closet. To make buyers feel they were getting value for money, we transformed it back into a bedroom. Then I hit a brick wall. Sabrina refused point-blank to move her parrots out of the master bedroom. Defeated, I cleared the clutter, cleaned the room and moved the TV so at least that wasn't the first thing to be seen on entering the room.

Sabrina wasn't convinced by my presentation of her house. She felt I'd removed its soul. But I knew that, to achieve a sale, we needed to depersonalise and show the cottage off in a way that would appeal to people wanting a home with real period charm.

And the result? One transformed cottage, renewed interest in the property and only one broken fingernail.

DIAGNOSIS

The interior of this house had gone to the dogs in every sense. The owner had simply lost all interest in the property and was just waiting to move on, while her two dogs were much in evidence. When selling up, it's essential that the house shouldn't look neglected, however disinterested in it you may have become. And superficial neglect may well imply to a buyer that more significant things could have been overlooked in the house. Here the kitchen operated as a combined kitchen/diner, but one which was too small to take much furniture. There's not much point to a breakfast bar if there's no room for the stools. In their place was a pile of wooden flooring that had lain there for a month. The kitchen units looked old-fashioned, hitting the eye with their dark wood and distracting from the rest of the room. And as for the view...

KITCHEN 4 BEFORE & AFTER

DOCTOR'S ORDERS

The dated, gloomy units were dragged into the twenty-first century by painting them a fresh white (Top Tip 4). Then we had to heavily edit the owner's possessions, which were in danger of crowding any viewer out of the room (Top Tip 2). Showcasing a few pieces of her glass and chinaware on the shelves and decluttering the work surfaces gave an impression of extra space.

We put the wood-effect flooring to good use in the dining area and removed some of the furniture, which gave us enough space for the much-needed bar stools.

Impossible to see, but very present, was the smell of dogs. When selling your house, you must clear up evidence of your pets (Top Tip 9). If you can't house them elsewhere, wash their bedding and, of course, the pets themselves. Many people don't like pets and yours may prevent them from seeing your home positively.

The outside of your house is just as important from inside. With a view like this, who'd want to sit at the breakfast bar? A new fence, some plants, and a new shed made all the difference.

Edit down your possessions to show them off and create a sense of space.

White paint can completely change the look of a dingy, dated kitchen.

Remember what can be seen through the windows. Tidy up outside, too.

KITCHEN 5 BEFORE & AFTER

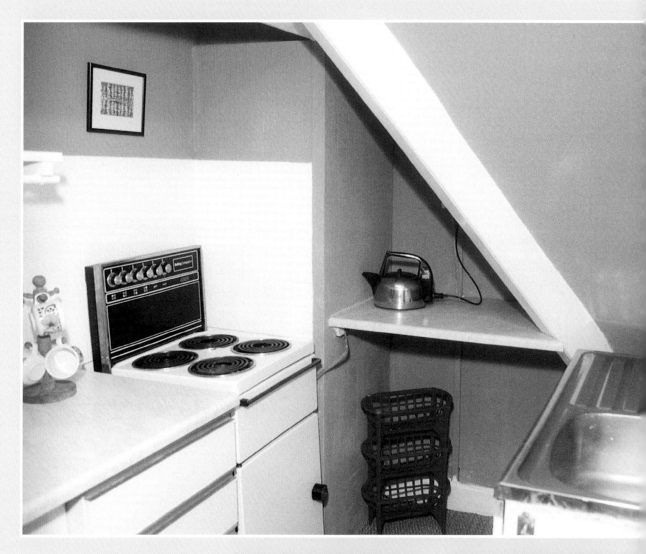

White can be too cold on the walls. It's easy and effective to paint it with something warmer.

Make sure you clear away all inessential items that are cluttering up the work surfaces.

DIAGNOSIS

This kitchen was small all right, but did it have to look quite so unloved and underused? The white walls made it feel like the inside of an igloo, while the washing-up and inessential clutter on the worktops was very dispiriting. The rubbish bin and the used dish towel did little to help matters. When I talk about depersonalising a room, I never mean stripping away every ounce of personality in it. My job was to put some back in here.

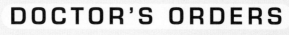

DOCTOR'S ORDERS

There's not a lot you can do when your kitchen's this size. But the obvious thing is to clean up. Surfaces should gleam and every bit of inessential clutter should be put away (Top Tips 1 and 2). No one wants to know if you've had a friend over for coffee the night before and no one cares which products you use to clean the place.

I felt that it was essential to warm the place up, which we did partly by introducing colour on the walls (Top Tip 3). Otherwise it was just a case of presenting the kitchen better. With the rubbish bin removed and a bright red vegetable rack in its place, things were cheering up. A lush plant put some life back into the space.

I removed the worn oven glove and dish towel altogether, leaving out only a mug tree and a kettle. My one other finishing touch was the addition of a picture, which I felt helped inject a little more personality into what had been a completely cheerless room.

all the elbow grease you muster to ensure that y surface shines.

Introduce a bright splash of colour by using a few carefully chosen accessories.

LIVING ROOMS

The living room can show signs of too much life. If your buyer is going to be able to mentally move his own things in, you've got to make it easy for him by removing too much evidence of yourself and emphasising the room's potential.

Breathe some fresh air into the room by repainting or re-papering it in a warm, but neutral colour. If the carpet's worn or has absorbed the smell of your pets, replace it. Again, a neutral colour is ideal. You can always brighten things up with a rug or two, which can go with you when you move.

Favourite ornaments and family photographs must all be thinned out to a bare minimum. If you can move the TV to a more discreet spot, then do so. You may love music, but must your CD collection cover the floor when there's all sorts of reasonably priced racking available? Weed out your crowded bookshelves. They don't have to be stuffed with books – use them to showcase special ornaments.

Make the most of the focal point in the room. Fireplaces should be swept and mantelpieces cleared of all but a couple of items. If you have a particularly old-fashioned heater, investigate replacing it with something more up-to-date. Hang a mirror or picture above the fireplace to emphasise its importance as a feature in the room. A blazing fire always looks welcoming, but remember to empty the grate when it's out. If the room looks over the garden and surrounding countryside, frame the windows with curtains and make sure nothing in the room blocks out the view.

There should be easy passage through the room, so check the door isn't obstructed and that French windows are easily accessible. Don't crowd the room with furniture or line it up around the walls – both make the room appear small and unwelcoming. Use the space to its best advantage.

Finish with a few well-chosen accessories in your accent colours – cushions, a rug, flowers (real ones), pot-pourri and candles will all help the transformation into a comfortable and desirable room.

TOP 10 TIPS
FOR THE LIVING ROOM

1 Hide all your family photos, golfing trophies or framed certificates. They only distract the viewers' attention away from the room and prevent them from making the crucial leap of seeing themselves living there.

2 Pay attention to the windows. Clean them, take away clutter that's obstructing the view and frame them with well-hung curtains or blinds.

3 Make a focal point of the fireplace, a special furniture grouping or even an interesting piece of art.

4 Tidy up the bookshelves. Group books in size order for a feeling of uniformity. To create a sense of space, leave room for one or two ornaments.

5 Arrange the furniture so there's easy passage through the room.

6 Having all the furniture lined up around the walls only makes the room look smaller and unwelcoming.

7 Good lighting can enhance the space and show off the room at its best.

8 Remove all evidence of pets and children. If that means removing the carpet too, then do it.

9 Don't forget to add finishing touches. Colour and life can be brought into the room by judicious use of cushions, rugs, pictures and flowers. Be careful not to overdo it, though.

10 Hide ugly radiators by boxing them in. This also provides a useful shelf for displaying one or two of your favourite ornaments.

LIVING ROOM 1 BEFORE & AFTER

Get rid of anything that particularly reflects your personality – however painful it may be!

Pay attention to the lighting and lampshades in a room. They can add style and atmosphere.

DIAGNOSIS

This room was set in a stunning period property, where a buyer had every reason to expect grandeur. Despite this I felt the living room lacked a necessary sense of comfort. The way that the furniture was arranged made the space seem smaller than it was. The blood-red walls and the furnishings at the window area were too strong and personal. They drew the eye away from everything else in the room. The roller blinds hardly did justice to such a wonderful bay either.

DOCTOR'S ORDERS

In general, this house wasn't on the critical list, but because the price was high, buyers would be picky so I needed to pay attention to the detail. The window was an important feature in the room, but I felt it was underexploited. Bright red obviously appealed to the owner, but it could easily have been offputting to a number of buyers who might not want to embark on a repainting job. A harmonious palette is generally more appealing. So I toned the area down with a light green that blended in with the rest of the room.

The windows themselves were imposing enough to deserve special treatment. This time we went to the expense of ordering custom-made blinds, which transformed the bay into a more elegant and inviting spot (Top Tip 2).

I went on a search-and-discover mission in the rest of the house, finding beautiful pieces of furniture that suited this room better. By moving the existing furniture around (Top Tip 5), removing some and thinning the contents of the shelves right out (Top Tip 4), the room immediately felt larger. The decorated cabinet and mirror made a delightful vignette against a difficult wall, the mirror helping to create the illusion of space.

Move furniture round until the area looks less small and crowded. Pieces from other rooms may help.

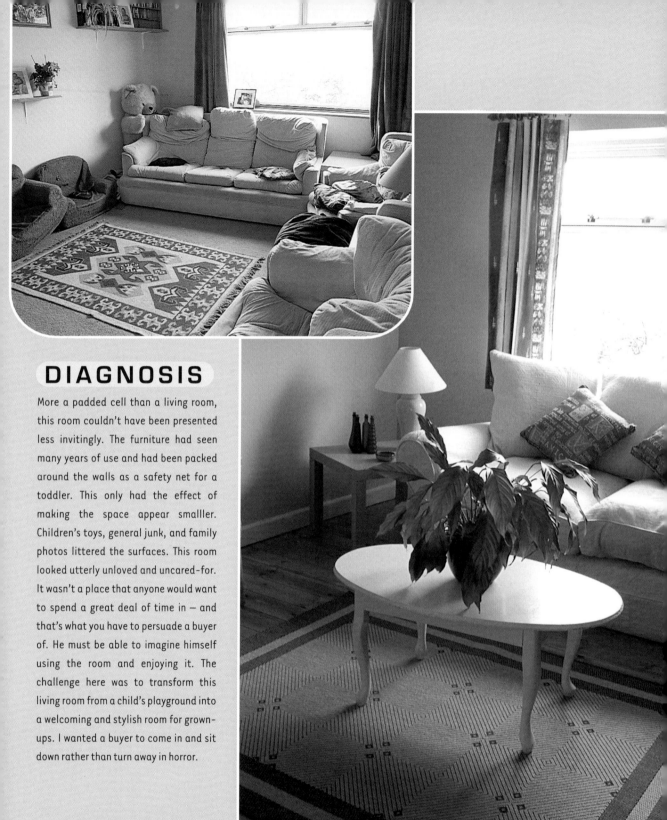

DIAGNOSIS

More a padded cell than a living room, this room couldn't have been presented less invitingly. The furniture had seen many years of use and had been packed around the walls as a safety net for a toddler. This only had the effect of making the space appear smalller. Children's toys, general junk, and family photos littered the surfaces. This room looked utterly unloved and uncared-for. It wasn't a place that anyone would want to spend a great deal of time in — and that's what you have to persuade a buyer of. He must be able to imagine himself using the room and enjoying it. The challenge here was to transform this living room from a child's playground into a welcoming and stylish room for grown-ups. I wanted a buyer to come in and sit down rather than turn away in horror.

LIVING ROOM 2 BEFORE & AFTER

DOCTOR'S ORDERS

The carpet had seen far better days, but underneath it the existing floorboards were in a good enough condition to sand and varnish — a cheap, but effective solution. Wood has a natural warmth which suits almost any room. The walls were then repainted a light, fresh shade of green.

The furniture had a left-over hippy feel to it and its arrangement was making the room look smaller than it was, so I decided to replace it with something more up-to-the-minute (Top Tip 6). If there's a real problem with the furniture in a room, I usually try to use other pieces from elsewhere in the house. In this case, I was unlucky. The piano came in from the dining room but the owners had to be persuaded to invest in a new sofa, table and rug, all of which would suit their new home, too.

Key to everything was colour-coordinating the accessories so the dark green accents of the curtains, cushions and plant tied together the different surfaces. Using dark accents against a pale background added depth and unity to the room (Top Tip 9).

Remember, new furniture often looks better and can go to your new home.

Look under a worn carpet to see if the floorboards are suitable for sanding.

Colour-coordinate carefully, using one colour as a base.

LIVING ROOM 3 BEFORE & AFTER

Dejunk thoroughly. Too much clutter will distract a buyer from seeing the properties of the room.

Unearth forgotten ornaments from your cupboards and showcase them on newly cleared shelves.

TVs can dominate a room so it's a good idea to remove them or hide them away in a cupboard.

DIAGNOSIS

The vivid blue here was overwhelming and did nothing for the room. The same went for the amount of clutter that was crammed in. Result: the living room looked tiny and cramped, giving away more about the owner's lifestyle than one needed to know. The room lacked a focal point and the absence of a dining area was a big minus point. My job was to clearly define the separate areas of the room and neutralise the colours while the owner cleared up the mess.

DOCTOR'S ORDERS

First to go were the blue walls, soon painted a soft peach to make the dark room seem larger and lighter. Clutter was another problem that was less easily solved. The owner had lived there with his girlfriend until they split up some months earlier. At first, he was reluctant to get rid of all sorts of things which belonged to their former life together but with a little persuasion, he was soon attacking the project with relish (Top Tip 1). The shelves in the alcove needed drastic thinning out, leaving only one or two striking ornaments (Top Tip 4). As the TV dominated the room, I had a simple cupboard built to house it, with the two speakers neatly on either side. Now we had a focal point (Top Tip 3).

Moving the furniture round allowed enough room for a dining area (Top Tip 5). A small table and two chairs fitted perfectly into the space that was freed between the kitchen and living areas. A clean, ironed tablecloth and a vase of fresh flowers completed the look.

Having cleared the clutter from the whole room, it was possible to see what else was needed to present it in the best possible way. Although we painted the walls, I retained the colour blue as a contrast. The room was tied together by buying some checked cushions, a rug and a coffee table that fitted in with the lighter, more modern feel of the room. Healthy green plants from the local garden centre provided a finishing touch of life and colour (Top Tip 9).

DIAGNOSIS

I had my work cut out to restore the rural charm this room had lost. It now looked dingy, depressing and out of date. The obvious problem was the massive, brick fireplace which completely dominated the room, making it seem narrower and darker. The deep red carpet and curtains only contributed to the same feeling. Clutter had accumulated on every surface, including the firegrate. Family photographs displayed on the window ledge took attention from the rest of the room and from the view outside. What I had to do was somehow reduce the effect of the chimney and generally lighten and brighten the room to give it a more modern aspect.

LIVING ROOM 4 BEFORE & AFTER

DOCTOR'S ORDERS

My chief concern here was the fireplace. I wanted to reduce the effect of the heavy red brick so I painted it with a mix of watered-down white emulsion before sanding it back to give a rustic, weathered appearance. This was an extremely cost-effective trick which made the fireplace apparently recede and the room seem bigger. Hanging a circular mirror on the chimney breast broke up its dominant, angular lines and helped to create the illusion of more space and light (Top Tip 3).

The carpet was a no-no. It was far too dark in combination with the blue chairs but, more importantly still, it smelled of dog. Invisible, but a real turn-off for many viewers (Top Tip 8). The curtains that teamed up with the carpet looked too Gothic to me and did nothing for the light in the room, so we replaced them with very simple cream curtains. Some toning cream or cream-and-blue cushions provided the final lift to the room.

Crucial too, was clearing the clutter and cleaning the surfaces (Top Tip 1). Immediately the room looked more attractive and with the addition of some plants, my job was done.

Investigate simple solutions to transform a dominant feature.

Invest in a new carpet to replace one that is worn, smelly or far too vivid.

Remove the family photos. Buyers want to see your house, not your life history.

CASE STUDY DULWICH

To achieve a sense of light and space, the deep blue and aquamarine colour scheme was repainted light sand and grey.

Dulwich is a leafy suburb of south London that is within easy reach of the city. It's an extremely sought-after area, where properties sell quickly. So why had Liz Maxwell's four-bedroom Victorian house complete with many original features, been on the market for four months?

I felt she wasn't showing the house to its full potential. The spacious rooms looked small because of the strong colours she'd chosen for the walls. I prefer colours to be used as accents against a more neutral background. The dining room was not presented well because it was doubling as a bedroom for her parents, so we moved them into one of the boys' rooms while they shared. Here, the garden resembled a football pitch instead of the desirable commodity it is in this part of the

world. With these things in mind, I set to work. The deep red hall was dark and claustrophobic, but nothing a few coats of cream paint, a new carpet, and a mirror couldn't put right. We had to unstick the door of the living room first before we could go on to tackle its overwhelming orange walls, toning them down to a lighter shade, using the brighter orange as an accent in the cushions and flowers, and taking our lead from the picture above the fireplace. I rearranged the furniture, removing one sofa, so that the room didn't look overcrowded. Once Liz's parents had moved upstairs, I could redefine the dining room. After all, this is the land of entertaining and dinner parties, and buyers will want to know they can join in. We removed the carpet to sand and varnish the floorboards. The yellow walls were painted a soft pistachio green, which immediately made the original features in the room stand out. We installed a dining table and chairs, and made a focal point of the fireplace with a picture above it, flowers in the grate and a couple of ornaments on the mantle shelf. Downstairs, the kitchen was the most tell-tale room. The deep blue and sea-green colour scheme only made the room appear smaller than it really was and the whole place needed a really good clean if a buyer wasn't going to leave with the impression that they'd have to incur the expense of refitting the whole room. I decided that it was worth investing in a new hob and taps to give a better impression of a working kitchen. The other vital change was to make sure the lighting worked effectively.

There wasn't much wrong with upstairs. I felt that reinventing the ground floor was enough to attract any potential buyer. But I hadn't forgotten the outside of the house. The front door was spruced up with a lick of paint and the football pitch at the back was returfed and the boys were banned from further matches until the house was sold. Two weeks after I left, it was.

Once Liz's parents had been found a bedroom upstairs, the dining room could be properly staged as an elegant place for entertaining – an asset to any home.

Liz Maxwell lived in Dulwich with her three sons. She was anxious to move nearer to their school and by selling the house she would also release some equity with which to fund her university studies. But after four months, sadly she had yet to receive a single offer.

CASE STUDY BRIXTON

Will Lusty had split up with his girlfriend, Steff Roberts, some months earlier. Still great friends, they wanted to sell the flat and move on but since she had moved out, standards had slipped and the flat had been stuck on the market for eight months.

House prices have rocketed in south London's Brixton. Now a popular place to live, it's in easy reach of central London and houses sell swiftly. That's unless they've been neglected for eight months like Will Lusty's and Steff Roberts' flat. This was one of the worst bachelor pads I'd ever seen.

Before reaching the flat, I had to go through a dingy communal hall crowded with bicycles, an old bed, old mail and dirt. First impressions are vital so we cleaned up, provided a mailbox and a welcome mat. Simple, but it gives a sound subliminal message. The flat itself was a good size but buried under a mass of clutter that had to be cleared. Peeling wallpaper and the unfinished ceiling in the narrow hallway had to be replaced and finished. The space was better balanced by using a darker colour below the dado rail. I also found a mirror in the garden, which we framed and hung to give an impression of space. Will

had created an office space at the end of the corridor, which only made the place feel more confined, so we cleared the box room and presented it as a proper office while vignetting a study area in the hall, which made the area look much bigger.

The kitchen was an abomination. Not only was it filthy and untidy, but it had an uninviting view of next door's wall, too. Will cleaned and recleaned it until it sparkled. We disguised the miserable view but kept the light by sticking some frosted etch-effect vinyl over the glass. It was too expensive to replace the units so we made the best of the room by repainting it a fresh light green and replacing the dead light bulbs. By the time we'd finished, it looked much improved.

The living room was quite simple to deal with. It was a good-sized room with a nice floor so, after removing the mess, we

The kitchen was cleaned and decluttered. To hide the unappealing view, the window was covered in etch-effect vinyl.

painted the walls beige and rearranged the furniture to create a specific sitting area as well as space for a dining table. We boxed in the radiator before I brought the whole room together by concentrating on the black-and-red accents.

All we had to do with the master bedroom was represent it by tidying and re-situating the furniture to give more space. I used Feng Shui techniques to position the bed diagonally across from the door with the headboard against the wall, keeping the whole room as uncluttered as possible. Much worse was the bathroom, so grimy it was embarrassing. A good clean, a coat of paint to warm the walls, and new pebble-effect vinyl tiles on the floor.

When we'd finished, I felt the flat was far more likely to appeal to the young professionals hunting for a home in Brixton. Will and Steff were confident they'd be receiving an offer soon.

The living room was improved by moving the furniture to create a central seating area, boxing in the radiator and tidying up the garden to provide more attractive outlook.

DIAGNOSIS

When I saw this room, I realised I would have to get rid of the different colours and patterns. The overall effect was too busy and disorienting. Pretty, antediluvian sofas were disguised by the throws and looked tatty too. The carpet was tired and worn and suffered from my pet no-no — doggy odour. Nets and floral curtains hardly did justice to the window. It was time for a thorough makeover here.

LIVING ROOM 5 BEFORE & AFTER

DOCTOR'S ORDERS

The owner and her dogs were particularly fond of this room but sadly, that didn't make it a selling point. Although she was unaware of the doggy odour, it was the first thing that struck me. Over time, it can be absorbed into carpet and furnishing fabric. The only way to get rid of it is to replace them altogether (Top Tip 8).

I decided on a much more neutral colour scheme, with the walls painted in two shades of cream above and below the dado rail, and a new grey carpet. We bought a new cream sofa that fitted perfectly into the window bay. These windows didn't need their old-fashioned curtains or another of my hates, the nets. They were replaced by white Roman blinds ,which I deliberately hung at different lengths to disguise the worst bits of the view (Top Tip 2).

In the rest of the room, I created a focal point out of the dated fireplace by painting the surrounding masonry white and hanging a large mirror above it (Top Tip 3). With a few carefully chosen pictures on the wall, grey and cream toning cushions on the sofa, and a simple coffee table, the room was ready to be shown (Top Tip 9).

Avoid net curtains. They are rather old fashioned and look terrible as soon as they get even slightly dirty. Instead find a way to dress the window that will hide the worst of the view while letting in light.

Too many colours and patterns make it impossible to focus on the whole of the room.

Keep things simple for an airy, modern feel which will appeal to most buyers.

DIAGNOSIS

The estate agent had warned me that this sitting room was not presented at its best. Certainly, the first thing I saw when I walked in was an old Christmas tree stuffed behind the sofa and then the general mess — bad Feng Shui all round. The owner had painted the room herself but in an gaudy orange which detracted from the more sophisticated atmosphere that a room like this should possess. And the fireplace was hidden beneath an array of nick-nacks completely covering both shelves. Original features in a period house are almost always deemed selling points so it's wise to show them off. The TV and videos dominated one corner of the room which presented a problem because there was no obvious place to hide them. I wasn't convinced that the rug was doing much for the room either, except making it seem smaller. This was a case of taking the family out before I could put the elegance back in.

LIVING ROOM 6 BEFORE & AFTER

DOCTOR'S ORDERS

First, we had to get rid of that ugly orange and repaint with a gentler, more subtle shade. Most importantly though, this room needed a really good clear out. Buyers have to be helped to make the mental leap of imagining themselves living somewhere new. It's too easy for them to think, 'They live like this? I can't,' and to walk out. The good points of this room were lost under the clutter (Top Tip 1). Once the mantelpiece was cleared, I made an elegant focal point by adding some candles and a bunch of fresh flowers with a mirror hung above (Top Tip 3).

I wanted to hide the television but with no suitable cupboard I decided on a screen. To make this, I hinged together the sides of an inexpensive flat-pack shelving unit and stapled the fabric over them. A simple, but effective solution to covering an eyesore. I had enough fabric left over to cover a small footstool, which helped to unify the room and add colour (Top Tip 9).

In the basement I found some fabulous antique furniture which I moved in here to give the room a more sophisticated, adult look. Peaceful and spacious, it was now seen at its best.

Hide unattractive objects or features behind a simple hand-made screen.

Bamboo blinds ensure privacy while letting the light flood into a room.

Candles add to the ambience. New ones look better than half-burnt ones.

Too much clutter means that the size and proportions of the room are lost from view.

Plump up cushions so that the room looks all the more welcoming.

A well-chosen plant adds life, colour and movement to an otherwise static corner.

DIAGNOSIS

The amount of possessions crowded into this room was horrifying. There wasn't an inch of space left. So much stuff detracted from the two crucial selling points: the original beams and the size of the room itself. Too much furniture only added to that effect.

The two sofas looked comfortable, if a little untidy, while the coffee table needed dressing up. Introducing some peace would restore some of the room's lost rustic charm.

DOCTOR'S ORDERS

The most vital thing to do in this room was to get rid of the extraordinary amount of clutter (Top Tip 1). Some went into storage, some was thrown away and some went into the owners' garage sale. Immediately the room seemed to literally expand and became much lighter.

Other than that, there wasn't an awful lot else to do. The enormous fan gave the impression that the room might become unpleasantly hot in summer. Why put the idea into viewers' heads, particularly when they might enjoy a higher tolerance of heat? It's always worth taking an objective look around a room to see what subliminal messages you might be giving by mistake. Burglar alarms, humidifiers, fans, extra heaters — these are the sort of things that can suggest problems to a buyer without them realising exactly quite why. Yet they are usually reasonably easy to disguise or put away. In place of the fan, I chose a large palm to add some vitality and movement to the room.

To make the space appear more comfortable and cared for, I plumped up the sofa cushions. They always look more inviting like this than squashed from the weight of endless bodies that have sprawled all over them. The coffee table looked lost between the sofas so, having polished it, I covered it with a lace cloth and a vase of flowers, which gave some focus to the area (Top Tip 9).

It only took a little thought to restore the room's rustic charm and to make it feel much larger, lighter and brighter than before. Presenting it like this means it must appeal to the greatest number of viewers.

Bring the two sides of a room together by making a focal point of a central coffee table.

DINING ROOMS

The dining room is often one of the most under-utilised rooms in the house. It may double as anything from a home office to a children's playroom or even a temporary bedroom. But that's not what potential buyers want to see. By smartening up your dining room and defining its function, you will give people an opportunity to imagine what life might be like if they buy your house. Remember, staging your home is all about promoting and selling a lifestyle.

Declutter and clean the room thoroughly first. You must make it look inviting, warm and sophisticated. Its purpose should be immediately obvious. If the walls are overpowering or shabby, repaint them in a safely neutral colour. A bright green carpet won't be to everyone's taste. Replace it with something more neutral or, if the floorboards are sound, sand and varnish the surface, using a mixture of sawdust and specialist sealing compound to fill any gaps. Keep the furniture in the room to a minimum so that it's possible to walk around or sit at the table with ease. If your table has doubled as a desk or a work surface, you might cover it with a smart tablecloth or runner.

Look at your dining room chairs. If you can, make sure they match and that the seat covers are not showing the remains of previous parties. Making new seat covers for loose seats is an inexpensive and simple job. Simple cushions are another way to give an impression of comfort. The fabric should tie in with the colours of the curtains or even repeat it. It's a good idea to lay the table but make sure you use your best matching china, glasses, cutlery and napkins. Anything less will look untidy and uninviting. Go for a simple vase of flowers instead.

If your house lacks a dining room, try and define a space for one instead. This may mean giving up a small area in the kitchen, living room or even the hall. To underline your message, lay the table simply but elegantly so it's clear where eating and entertaining can be enjoyed. Believe me, if you pay attention to these important details, you will add to the intrinsic value of your home.

TOP TIPS
FOR THE DINING ROOM

1 If you are fortunate enough to have a separate dining room, don't let it double as an office, play room or box room while your home is being marketed.

2 Avoid clutter, especially on the table and tops of furniture, so that people will find it easy to imagine themselves sitting down to enjoy a meal there.

3 If you need to freshen up the walls choose colours that are warm and invite dining and entertaining. If using wallpaper, be sure that it is not too busy or overpowering.

4 Don't crowd the room with furniture. It should be easy to walk round the table.

5 Freshen up old dining chairs with smart new seat covers or add small, comfortable cushions.

6 Cover a particularly tatty table with a new tablecloth or table runner.

7 If there is no separate dining room, find a space which could be used as a dining area and define it with table and chairs.

8 If you haven't got a table and chairs, beg, borrow or hire them – this is an essential part of selling a lifestyle.

9 Fresh flowers in a beautiful vase in the centre of the table will give it focus.

10 Lay the table with coordinating napkins and china, issuing a subliminal invitation to your viewer, but keep it simple, please.

DINING ROOM 1 BEFORE & AFTER

Strident background colours are out. They make the room seem smaller and may put off a buyer.

Plants must be in tip-top condition. Anything less looks untidy and uncared for.

Allow as much light into the room as possible. Clean all windows and glass partitions thoroughly.

DIAGNOSIS

That green carpet must be one of the brightest I've ever seen during my whole time as House Doctor. Although the owner was keen on golf, having your own putting green indoors is going too far. It dominated the room and could make any buyer turn tail. Otherwise I felt the room was too crowded with the owner's personality. I wasn't keen on the rather leggy plant that was climbing the trellis or the unattractive pot and dish that it was planted in.

DOCTOR'S ORDERS

Not surprisingly, the carpet had to go. Since the walls were already a restful neutral colour, we were able to compromise on a less strident green on the floor. The dining table and chairs were in good condition and tied in with the dresser and sideboard.

It wasn't a big room and I felt that the number of family photographs accumulated on top of the piano made it seem smaller (Top Tip 2). Certainly they immediately drew attention away from anything else. I always like to depersonalise a room as much as possible when selling a house. It makes it easier for the buyer to mentally move in. Instead we made a more elegant vignette by adding two pictures and a pretty vase, which I'd found elsewhere in the house. I moved the music stand simply because I felt it was better located closer to the piano. Opening the sheet music gave the impression that the room was often used.

The plant did nothing except provide an obstacle to manoeuvre round. Without it, we could remove the trellis and leave the frosted glass, which lent a sense of connection with the adjoining room without it destroying the sense of intimacy in the dining room. The bare and uninviting table was soon improved by the addition of a flowering plant that toned in with the chair seats and curtains and gave focus (Top Tip 9).

House doctoring does not have to mean complete upheaval. This was an example of how a few minor adjustments can be more than enough to inject an indifferent room with a real touch of class in a short space of time.

Edit or remove possessions that will distract the buyer from looking at the room as a whole.

DIAGNOSIS

Busy, busy, busy was the overwhelming first impression of this dining room, swiftly followed by the feeling of a rather dark and dingy place. The carpet was the owner's favourite, but the pattern was so strong that it ran the risk of repelling any viewer. On one wall the wallpaper had a particularly fussy bird design, which made the room appear smaller. Against it stood an ugly 1950s cabinet, stuffed with glass and china, as were the cupboards on the other side of the room. The sideboard was groaning under the weight of all sorts of bits and pieces, including a vase of unattractive dried flowers. Above, the wall was scatter-shot with decorative plates. The dining chairs were a mismatch of high- and low-backs, while the lace tablecloth just added to the general sense of confusion. My job here was to make the room realise its potential, lightening and brightening it, and using furniture from only one period.

DINING ROOM 2 BEFORE & AFTER

DOCTOR'S ORDERS

I removed the cabinet and the armchair to give more space before moving the sideboard to rest another wall. The walls were stripped and a dado rail added. I chose anaglypta paper below because it's hardwearing and can hide a multitude of sins with a muted heritage paint below and a paler shade above (Top Tip 3).

The carpet was removed under the owners' protest and replaced with seagrass matting which I find is a cost-effective solution to flooring in any period of house. It's warm and hardwearing, too.

I removed the plates from the wall and instead, hung a large picture in colours that toned in with the rest of the room. The antique china and glass bursting from the cupboards was dramatically thinned down and only a few pieces were kept, which could be showcased properly (Top Tip 2). The table was in tip-top condition, a beautiful piece of furniture that looked much better displayed without a tablecloth, but polished and dressed up with period candlesticks and a posy of fresh flowers (Top Tip 9). I took away the shorter-backed chairs and left the room uniform in character and looking twice its original size.

Use a dado rail to break up an expanse of wall and add to the period feel.

Always choose fresh flowers for their scent and the vitality they give to a room.

If you have good pieces of furniture, show them off. Don't forget the polish.

DINING ROOM 3 BEFORE & AFTER

Messy multi-functional rooms
don't cut it with buyers. They want
to see what the room is used for.

If the right furniture can't be found,
buy, borrow or hire something until
the property is sold.

DIAGNOSIS

Who would believe this was a dining room? It had a little bit of everything — wine cellar, office, playroom. This is no way to present any room. The function of each room in the home must be clearly spelled out. A dining room is particularly important because it implies that a certain kind of desirable lifestyle is on offer. But not here. This was a clear case of having to define the dining room so that it would add value to the house by giving it that extra space.

DOCTOR'S ORDERS

A dining room should be sophisticated, relaxing — a room conducive to enjoyment and fulfilment of the senses. Attention should be clearly focussed on the table, with little distraction from elsewhere (Top Tip 1). This messy, multi-functional room had to be completely cleared and the walls painted a soothing neutral shade, while the carpet was replaced with another, more suitable, one.

We boxed up all the files and clutter and then, with an empty room to furnish, we went shopping. The owners had no appropriate furniture so for once we could start from scratch. After a good look round, they settled on a light wood table and chairs, which they felt would fit into their new house but in the meantime, fitted the bill perfectly here (Top Tip 8).

The rest of the furniture they bought included two maple bookcases and a maple work station, which could be placed discreetly in a corner. I was reluctant to include this but gave in under pressure, given the promise that they would keep it super-tidy.

Before, the room had seemed much darker and smaller than it really was. Although the new wall colours, carpet and furniture went a long way towards addressing that, I had to pay attention to the large window, too. Moving the table into the centre of the room meant that the window was no longer blocked (Top Tip 4). Having ruthlessly cleaned it, we then hung some new curtains in a light, floral fabric. They took the heavy feeling away from the window and visually linked the room to what was going on outside.

Using pale colours can make a room seem to double in size.

CASE STUDY SUTTON-IN-ASHFIELD

Although Janet Clare's two-bedroomed home was pleasantly situated on a corner site in central Sutton-in-Ashfield, a town close to the M1 and Sherwood Forest, there was clearly some sort of problem here: it had already been languishing on the market for five months.

My diagnosis was swift. Although Janet's dogs were her life, we had to de-dog the house if it was to appeal to the majority of buyers. Don't get me wrong. I love dogs but I wouldn't want to live in a kennel. Despite all Janet's objections, I wanted to contain them to a smaller area just while she sold her house. The property had real expansion potential to be a family home and that had to be made more obvious. We converted the 30-foot outdoor conservatory at the back of the house into a huge kennel. With the dogs elsewhere, we could then begin work.

Carpets always retain the smell of dog so those in the hall and second bedroom, which doubled up as a dog's room, had to go. I replaced them with sea-grass matting as it's so adaptable. The second bedroom was returned to its original purpose, the junk and the parrot cages being dispersed to the dump and the conservatory respectively. Then we started from scratch, painting, dressing with new bedlinen and putting blinds over the windows to hide the dogs, who were now in the

Janet Clare had moved to her two-bedroomed bungalow as a stop-gap until she found a bigger home for herself, her eleven dogs and three parrots. Now she wanted to move, but she couldn't find the right buyer.

greenhouse behind the bungalow. The final touch was the curtains. It was now obvious that Janet was selling a two-bedroomed property, not an expensive one-bedroomed one. In the master bedroom, it was just a question of getting rid of the surface clutter and buying new curtains and bedlinen to tie the room together.

Janet carefully supervised the packing of most of the gorgeous objects in the living room before we showcased those that were left. We painted the walls a slightly deeper shade of yellow than the hall walls, simultaneously uniting but differentiating the two rooms. The only remaining problem was the Macdonalds sign, clearly visible over the road. I used additional curtain fabric to make pelmets, which framed the window and hid the sign.

In the indoor conservatory Janet insisted on wipeable vinyl tiles — more practical with all those dogs — and a vibrant pink for the walls. The dogs' furniture was moved to their new room, so we could turn this into a proper conservatory with a tropical theme.

But sadly Janet was unhappy with the work, and she felt disappointed that it had removed the character from her home. I couldn't persuade her of the need to depersonalise your home when selling it, so the dogs were unpenned and her possessions reinstated. When we last heard from her, the property was still on the market.

The second bedroom was cleared of its doggy smells and musty carpet. With colour-coordinated bedlinen and curtains a junk room was transformed into a calm and appealing bedroom.

Janet had to be persuaded to remove some of her favourite personal objects from the lounge, so that the viewers would not be overwhelmed by her particular style.

DIAGNOSIS

The owner of this house loved antique collecting to the extent that she was being crowded out of her own home. When I walked into the dining room, I felt dizzy with the effect of all the things crammed in there. It was so bad that I completely missed the room itself. This woman had to be stopped. Having the table in the middle of the room meant that, although it could be easily got at, the fireplace was blocked from view. Attention was also taken away from it by the cluttered alcoves on either side. I'm never keen on lace tablecloths, which seem to me to be unnecessarily fussy. A combination of curtains and Viennese blinds was definitely too much of a good thing and made the room seem smaller. The task here was obvious. We had to be brutal about what was kept and what went into storage before we could show off the size of the room and its principal features.

DINING ROOM 4 BEFORE & AFTER

DOCTOR'S ORDERS

We freshened up the room and disguised the busy border with a couple of coats of paint in a delicate pinky white (Top Tip 3).

I had my work cut out to persuade the owner to sell, chuck out or store so many of her beloved antiques (Top Tip 2). After being told that she could only have six things displayed on the dresser, she had to be stopped from sneaking out more but eventually, she admitted that she felt liberated by decluttering herself so radically.

Placing the dining table against the wall wasn't ideal since it would have to be moved every meal time, but in this case we had to compromise so that the fireplace could be seen in all its glory. With the jumble edited right down on either side and a single picture on the mantel shelf, it became the rightful focal point.

The red curtains were quite unnecessary here and blocked out light from the room. Without them, the blind looked much better too. Removing the tablecloth and clutter meant that the furniture could be properly seen and admired. When we'd finished, the room appeared much lighter, airier and more inviting.

Fresh fruit always looks good. But remember to remove the sticky labels.

Make the most of the original features in a room. Don't block them with furniture.

Strictly limiting the number of items on shelves gives an impression of space.

DINING ROOM 5 BEFORE & AFTER

Disguise ugly radiators by boxing them in first, then create an attractive vignette.

Consider how to use furniture in different ways. A little imagination gave this table a new lease of life.

DIAGNOSIS

At the end of this L-shaped living room was an odd sitting area, where a long sofa faced a blank wall and a radiator. It felt just like a surgery waiting room. However, the biggest problem with this property was that it didn't have a formal dining room. This dead space would provide the ideal solution. With a change of furniture, a match of ceiling lights, and the removal of that ugly television, we would add an essential extra room to the property.

DOCTOR'S ORDERS

I wanted the new dining room to conform with the luxuriousness of the rest of the house. One of my pet hates is exposed radiators. There's something ugly and unfinished about them. Whenever I can, I recommend that they are boxed in. That's exactly what we did here, with the result that we could create a vignette, using the new shelf for two decorative candlesticks with a suitably wide picture above it.

The table came from outside, where it had languished with a broken marble top on the roof terrace (Top Tip 8). Leaving the marble up there, we had a new table top cut from MDF. Once we'd painted it black, it was coated in gold size, a specialist adhesive. Then I demonstrated how to brush on sheets of variegated green gold leaf before varnishing it. The result? A glitzy table that made a strong statement. Because the table itself was so arresting, I didn't think it needed laying. A plant in the centre was enough (Top Tip 9).

I changed the ceiling light to match the one in the adjoining living room and to visually link the two rooms. As for the rest, it was just a question of rustling up the furniture from elsewhere in the house and changing the pictures on the walls.

By so successfully defining a dining area (Top Tip 7), we added value to the house and created a room that many buyers would love to have as their own.

Pictures should be carefully chosen to complement one another and the area where they are hung.

BEDROOMS

The master bedroom is key to the way buyers will perceive your home. It's the most personal space in the house and you should consider spending up to £200 to make the most of it.

Maximise the space so the room looks as large as possible. Present the room in a way that will appeal to the greatest number of people. By day, it should be fresh, light and bright. Strident colours, patterns and floral prints on the walls are out. They make the room look smaller and may put off some buyers altogether. Walls and carpets should be replaced with warm, neutral shades where necessary.

Put away any clothes you've left lying around. If you share the room with your pets, now's the time to find them a new sleeping space.

Look at the way the furniture is arranged. Minimise the number of pieces or the space will seem cramped. The bed should be positioned so that it doesn't block the door or the window. Clear the top of the wardrobe of all junk and consider if it would be better placed against another wall.

It's worth investing in new bedlinen, which will look great and reinforce the impression that this is a house you've loved and taken care of. If you don't want the added expense, at least make sure that what you have is clean and ironed.

Take your colour scheme from something in the room, such as a picture, and plan your accents from that. Add a few finishing touches – perhaps cushions at the head of the bed or a throw, neatly folded at the foot; scented candles, pot-pourri or fresh flowers will add to the atmosphere, too.

If you're showing your room in the evening, make sure your lighting is effective. Directed right, it can help disguise the worst features by highlighting the best ones. Bedside lights are often more effective than a ceiling light. Check that all the lampshades are clean and the light bulbs are all working. Candles always give a flattering light and provide an enticing, romantic atmosphere. Make sure those buyers leave, wanting to come back soon.

TOP TIPS
FOR THE BEDROOM

1 Walls should be painted a warm, neutral colour, such as a soft peach, apricot or apple green. Strong colours and patterns may overwhelm a buyer and put them off.

2 Replace a worn carpet with a new one or, if the floorboards are in good condition, sand and stain them and invest in a couple of accent rugs.

3 Clear all clutter. But this is the one room where it is all right to display a few well-chosen personal photos.

4 Arrange the furniture so the room appears at its most spacious and maximum light comes through the window.

5 Make a feature of a window with a view, framing it with a pair of attractive colour-coordinated curtains.

6 Buy a set of new bedlinen or make sure the linen that you have is clean and ironed properly to give the impression that you care for your home.

7 If you're transforming a former junk room into a second bedroom and require a bed,

beg, borrow or even hire one until your sale is complete.

8 Complete the whole transformation with the addition of pot-pourri, scented candles or essential oils ... one scent per room, please.

9 However much you love your pets, remove them from the room. You may not notice their smell, but it can be extremely off-putting to potential buyers.

10 Check your lighting. Make sure the shades are clean, the bulbs work, and that the best features are highlighted.

BEDROOM 1 BEFORE & AFTER

Mirrors enhance the sense of space and light. Don't overdo them in a bedroom. It can be embarrassing.

Etch spray can be used to retain privacy, but admit light, too.

Pale colours contribute to the peaceful, harmonious atmosphere required in a bedroom.

DIAGNOSIS

What a depressing room! Dark, dreary and dreary and messy. A bedroom should always be presented as a sanctuary for privacy and relaxation. The colour that was chosen for the walls made this room feel claustrophobic, as did the painting on the wall (literally). A window looked out onto a brick wall, which only added to the sombre atmosphere, though a curtain or blind would only make things worse. Otherwise, the place just needed a thoroughly good clean and tidy.

DOCTOR'S ORDERS

To help the room to convey an impression of serenity and calm, I chose a delicate primrose yellow for the walls with white woodwork (Top Tip 1). Once that maddening red had gone, the atmosphere in the room changed and, even better, it seemed twice the size and much lighter. We bought some architectural drawings to be seen from the bed.

However, light was the next problem on the agenda (Top Tip 10). The closeness of the wall outside the window meant that not much natural light could find its way into the room. It also meant that there was absolutely no view. Rather than darken the room with curtains or blinds, I used a neat trick. I masked out a narrow outline round the edge of each pane and then sprayed the rest with etch spray. Meanwhile, I had an electrician fix up a weatherproof lamp outside to shine in through the window. The result was that light streamed in, but glare was reduced and privacy maintained by the etch effect.

The room was thoroughly tidied, leaving the mirror – which helped with the impression of space – and the desk and chair (Top Tip 3). I insisted the television was removed until the flat was sold. The pine furniture and floorboards suited the room well, giving it warmth without making it seem darker. A blanket chest looked better at the foot of the bed and the rug made getting out of bed look a little more comfortable.

New bedlinen always makes a huge difference to the appearance of the room (Top Tip 6), so with that and a new grey cushion, the bedroom was transformed into a peaceful haven that would attract any buyer.

DIAGNOSIS

It's just as important to stage secondary bedrooms properly as it is your master bedrooms. The more desirable space you seem to have, the better off you'll be. This bedroom was tucked away in the attic of a large family house. It had been let as student accommodation and was looking way past its best as a result. This bedroom, and the other three rooms that went with it, needed a drastic face-lift.

The room looked bleak and unlived-in. Icy white walls sent a shiver through me, while the furniture looked as though it had been dumped there years ago and forgotten. Bed bases were clearly visible and the children's duvet covers and pillowcases hardly spelled comfort. The carpet was stained and dirty, too.

I wanted to breathe life and warmth back in here so the attic floor would become a major selling point.

BEDROOM 2 BEFORE & AFTER

DOCTOR'S ORDERS

I got rid of the old furniture and the awful carpet that had seen much better days. To my delight, the floorboards were in good condition, so we primed them and painted them grey to tone in with the new warm beige walls (Top Tip 2).

Without wanting to crowd the room, we added two small shelving units on which to display a few chosen pieces and matching bedside lights (Top Tip 10).

The chest of drawers and mirror filled the chimney breast perfectly and made a notional division between the two sleeping spaces. New bedlinen made a huge difference, as did the rug in complementary warm colours (Top Tip 6).

My favourite addition in this room was covering foam cubes with felt to create cheap, but funky seats that tied in with the bedlinen and cushions.

Take the chill off the coldest room by painting the walls a more friendly colour.

For funky furniture, buy foam cubes and cover them in bright coloured felt.

Soften the effect of bare floorboards by adding a colourful, foot-warming rug.

BEDROOM 3 BEFORE & AFTER

Ban all evidence of untidy teenagers. Bag up their belongings and keep them out of sight.

Make the most of your master bedroom. It must convey a seductive air of calm and privacy.

Make every inch of space count by covering garish walls with light, soothing colours.

DIAGNOSIS

Where to begin? This master bedroom had mysteriously fallen into the hands of a teenage boy, who had turned it into a pit. To present one of the principal rooms of a house like this is madness. After some tough talking, we persuaded the boy to have a major clear-out, before being relegated to a secondary bedroom. That meant I could start from scratch and turn the master bedroom into somewhere where someone might actually want to spend the night.

DOCTOR'S ORDERS

If you don't define your rooms properly you will seriously devalue your property. In a house this size with a high asking-price, buyers had every right to expect an impressive master bedroom. Without it, the house gives the impression of being smaller than it really is. In the unlikely event of them being able to see past the mayhem to the room's potential, the last thing they'd want would be the unenviable task of stripping the walls. That had to be our job. But before we could begin, all that teenage detritus had to be junked (Top Tip 3). The recalcitrant teenager had to be convinced that his contribution would really help sell the house. At last, many bin-bags later, we were ready to begin. Wallpapering giant posters onto the walls may have seemed a good idea at the time, but it was extremely hard work to get them off again. Having finally succeeded, the walls were ready to be lined, then painted a soft country beige (Top Tip 1).

Those were the principal things that contributed to the transformation of the bedroom. After that, it was simply a question of finding the right furniture in the rest of the house and dressing the room so that it looked appropriately elegant and spacious. The only investment the owners had to make was in new bedlinen and curtains, which made the room much fresher and more inviting (Top Tip 6).

When we'd finished, none of us could believe it was the same room.

Coordinating cushions on the bed are a final touch that can bring the room together.

CASE STUDY FROME

American Ray Molho and his English partner Lynda Kramer lived in a Grade II listed property in the centre of Frome. They had decided to sell up and use the equity to go travelling, but their house had been stuck on the market for over five months.

Frome is a charming market town in Somerset, where stunning period properties can still be found at reasonable prices. Ray Molho and Lynda Kramer had bought the house to share with her father, but after his death they found the place too big for the two of them. At first I was baffled as to why they'd called me. The house had lots of history and character, and was presented almost perfectly. In fact, I'd almost have bought it there and then myself. The only thing that struck me was that the fireplace in the ground-floor living room needed attention. It had the potential of being a marvellous focal point but was blocked from view by a table and looked as if it wasn't working, which threw up a question mark about how much it would cost to repair. We unbricked it, fitted a pretty stove that I'd found at the local salvage yard, then dressed it with a mirror above and candles around it. Otherwise, the only other area that needed work

seemed to be the garden, which was under constant threat from rabbit. Some bright border plants helped but the key to making it a peaceful retreat with an appropriately period feel was the mirror that I made from an old stone window frame.

But it wasn't until I'd been through the house itself that I finally realised why their property was not selling. Ray took me out the back to see the villain of the piece — what had once been the stables had been converted into an epic living space. But the room had a real crisis of identity. Was it a ballroom, a bedroom or a bar? Looking at it, any buyer would feel that it could be a huge liability. I had to make it look more of a comfortable domestic space, in keeping with the rest of the house.

Having cleared out all of Ray and Lynda's personal clutter (except for their pet rabbit, which none of us could catch), we

**The new marmoleum floor gave the room a focus and introduced a
strong colour scheme, which brought the space together.**

set to work. A new marmoleum floor was the centrepiece and
defined the three areas of the room. Taking it as the basis for my
colour scheme, I chose a warm mustard for the side walls but a
deep red for the two end walls. This is a nifty trick to make the
space look smaller by apparently reducing its length. We took
down the ugly folding partitions but I retained a sense of division
using painted garden trellis. In the centre I created a disco/dance
space, complete with existing glitterball, by tenting the ceiling in
parachute silk. Wrought-iron wall sconces from the salvage yard
gave the finishing Gothic touch. The only thing left was the bar,
which I smartened up by painting it black and adding glasses and
accessories to define it and make it look more 'clubby'.

Happily, Ray and Lynda were soon able to put their revitalised
hall to good use when they celebrated the sale of their house with
a party just two weeks later.

**This epic space was not being shown to its real potential and
this was preventing an otherwise speedy sale. First, we had to
remove all trace of Ray and Lynda's personal items, including
the zebra-skin rug.**

CASE STUDY CRIEFF

Kairen Powell was about to turn fifty so had decided to give her life a shake-up by moving from the home where she had lived for the last twenty years. She was anxious to discover why buyers had not been flocking to her door.

Kairen Powell's split-level bungalow was in Crieff, Perthshire, a beautiful part of the world, but it had been on the market for an astonishing five years. Why?

For a start, the outside had nothing going for it. It was grey and forbidding, with no pulling power at all. To prevent any more buyers turning tail before they'd even crossed the threshold, we gave the exterior a bit of Swiss chalet chic by adding wooden shutters to the windows and painting them — and the front door — a sprightly shade of green. Once the garden had been tidied up, some hanging baskets and the washing line removed, things were soon starting to look up.

Inside, the dark and dated hall let the house down as much as the outside had. I liberated a parquet floor that we found beneath the tired old carpet and then ran new carpet up the stairs and along the landing. The ugly swirling wallpaper was replaced with a more modern, sophisticated design, which lightened the space and drew you into Kairen's home. Being in her dining room was like being on a superannuated putting green. I've never seen such a bright green shag-pile carpet. You've guessed it — it was replaced with a more subtle shade.

The living room and kitchen were a symphony in pink, Kairen's favourite colour. We repainted both, leaving the pink furniture in the living room and the pink tiles in the kitchen, but by using the colour as an accent, it became less overwhelming. It made sense not to replace the precarious brass hood over the fire but to put in a wooden mantelpiece, giving the fireplace greater presence on a long wall. We thinned out furniture and clutter, even removing the book jackets for a neater, more uniform look.

In the kitchen we defined a breakfast area and followed the green/pink colour scheme to give a subliminal invitation to buyers.

The kitchen needed to look fresher and cleaner. After elbow grease had improved the general appearance, we created an attractive breakfast area. The back door had been jammed for years, but it could suggest something had been hidden outside. Unblocking it and giving access to the back yard was essential.

Upstairs, the view from the master bedroom was improved by removing the washing line from the yard and adding some potted plants. But the bathroom needed much more work. The shag-pile carpet that even ran up the side of the bath looked better replaced by self-adhesive cork tiles. With the horrible flowery walls painted over to tone in with the suite and the clutter removed, the room had become somewhere anyone might enjoy using. One of our prospective buyers thought we'd transformed a dosshouse into a guest house. And sure enough, Kairen received an offer for the property the day after we left.

The dark and unwelcoming hallway and stairs were brightened up by replacing the worn stair carpet and by using a contemporary wallpaper with a patterned half-height border.

DIAGNOSIS

What a wasted opportunity this was. Here, a secondary bedroom was being used as the master bedroom but in any event, where was the sense of sanctuary? Who on earth would want to imagine themselves coming here after a hard day's work? I couldn't think of anywhere more unrelaxing to be. The place was full of clutter and horribly untidy. It was a nice gesture to put the bunch of fresh flowers out, except nobody could see them hidden behind, of all things, the ironing board. The wallpaper and the curtains were busy and distracting and they certainly didn't go well with the crumpled, stripey duvet cover.

I wanted to restore the room to its rightful position as a secondary bedroom before giving it a completely new look. Without exception, a bedroom must always be inviting, offering itself as a place of retreat with a soothing, peaceful atmosphere within.

BEDROOM 4 BEFORE & AFTER

DOCTOR'S ORDERS

Once we'd decided to get rid of the existing decoration, I decided that the room should have an airy blue colour scheme taken from the existing curtains and carpet (Top Tip 1). The walls were painted a cool blue and the new bedlinen set off by a toning throw.

My favourite change to the room came when we disguised the radiator. Using MDF, we built a cover — slashed to let the heat out — with a reasonable-sized storage chest in front of it. For the top of the chest, I covered a foam seat pad with blue fabric and added some contrasting cushions.

Without all the mess and the ironing board returned to its rightful place downstairs, the room could be seen for the decent size it was (Top Tip 3). I left the cheval mirror in the corner, where it was neatly out of the way but still served to increase the sense of space and, of course, provided a useful function in the room.

I didn't think a major outlay on furniture was necessary but the two large floor cushions gave an extra message of comfort and relaxation. What an improvement!

Make a simple storage chest from MDF, which can double as a seat.

Base a colour scheme on something in the room; in this case, the curtains.

A restful atmosphere is achieved here with a total absence of clutter.

BEDROOM 5 BEFORE & AFTER

A single picture can make a much stronger statement than a disparate group of three.

Dominant colours distract from other features in the room. It's always sensible to repaint them.

Matching bedside lights can create the impression of an intimate and peaceful place to be.

DIAGNOSIS

More an abattoir than a boudoir, this bedroom had me screaming in horror at the colour of the walls. The owner chose blue for the cupboards before realising the colours didn't go with each other. The windows were ineffectively draped with a piece of fabric that did nothing for them. The pictures on the chimney breast distracted the eye. A rumpled bed, a television and the chair — they all had to go. I had to realise the potential of a truly luxurious place of rest.

DOCTOR'S ORDERS

Taking my cue from the cupboards, I picked a blue-and-cream colour scheme for the room. It was a relief for everyone when the hideous red walls disappeared under several coats of a muted cream (Top Tip 1). The room looked bigger and the cupboards could be seen better.

The windows were a potential focal point but they were not being exploited to their full potential. The owner had some wonderful antique curtains but she simply hadn't hung them properly. In a house as splendid as this, we really needed to make the best of this feature, so we rehung the curtains in the correct way and instantly made a dramatic improvement to the whole appearance of the room.

To show off the new window treatment, I removed the ugly chair and television — I always think they create the wrong impression in a bedroom — replacing them with a stunning blue-and-white vase, and pushing back the small pile of stacking tables. The patterns in the fabrics and vase gave a slightly oriental feel to the room, which I decided to exploit by hanging the large elephant picture over the bed. Unlike the three pictures it replaced, it made a strong statement and brought the whole room together.

I was able to leave the lighting in the room just as it was. Apart from a central pendant light, it's always wise to have two bedside lights to create a sense of intimacy in the room (Top Tip 10). The owner was thrilled with the result and I dare bet she got the most restful night's sleep for some time, confident that she was now going to get a quick sale.

Dress windows correctly — if necessary, get advice on how to hang curtains properly.

DIAGNOSIS

Talk about a sad case of the blues! This bedroom had absolutely no pizzazz to it whatsoever. It looked like an unoccupied student pad. Presenting a room in this way does nothing towards getting a sale. Simply put: it doesn't look like an asset.

The first thing I saw was the ugly radiator and peeling paint. The carpet was old and stained and the beds didn't even match. The matching fabric for the duvet and curtains was a busy floral print, which looked dreadfully old-fashioned, as did the awful mob-cap lightshade, which wasn't even hung straight. I didn't like the way the curtain draped on the bed either. Although I'm always advocating mirrors, the one in this room was useless: not attractive nor practical unless you got on your hands and knees.

To make this room sell, I had to smarten it up first and then inject it with some much needed character.

BEDROOM 6 BEFORE & AFTER

DOCTOR'S ORDERS

Peeling paint is like a red flag to any buyer, suggesting that worse, unseen problems could be the cause. Why put the idea into anyone's head when all you have to do is give the room a lick of paint ? (Top Tip 1). With the room immediately looking fresher, we bought some new curtains that properly fitted the windows and blended in with the new bedspread.

I particularly liked the Gothic design of the bedhead, which introduced some softer, curving lines into the room. By choosing a double bed and reorientating the room as a result, we managed to hide the awful radiator. A larger, framed mirror — tall enough to use and to increase the sense of space — also did the job of partly hiding the central heating pipes in the room. The bedside table and chair were charity-shop finds.

I then personalised things with a few finishing touches — the coordinating lampshade, bedlinen and cushions, not forgetting the pretty bunch of flowers, which all confirmed it as a comfortable, lived-in room (Top Tip 8).

Highlighting an unusual feature can give a room a whole new personality.

Check the light shade. Make sure it's not crooked, dated or absent.

Colour-coordinate accessories to give a fresh, up-to-the-minute look.

BATHROOMS

Like kitchens, bathrooms must appear as completely clean, light and spacious as possible. They must look up-to-date. The idea of having to undertake expensive modifications is enough to put some buyers off. Improve the look of your suite by improving what's round it.

Get rid of strident colours or busy wallpaper with some repainting. If the tiles are what's letting the room down, repaint them with a specialist tile primer and paint – a very simple but effective cure.

Carpet soaks up water, with the result that it never looks its best and very often smells. There are lots of fabulous tiles that you could use instead, including sheets of beautiful mosaic.

You cannot apply too much elbow grease to the bath, basin and lavatory. If any enamel is chipped, it's easy to cover it up with specialist paint. New shower curtains always look better. Hide or throw out everything that's inessential here or half-used. All indispensable personal items should be safely stored away out of sight. If there are any small jobs you've never quite got round to, like the dripping tap, the broken loo seat or towel rail, fix them NOW.

Look at the treatment of the windows. Stick-on plastic etching can be an effective way of maintaining privacy while admitting light. Blinds should be kept clean and operational, and curtains unobtrusive. Make sure there's a light over the bathroom mirror and from the ceiling (operated from outside). Sometimes just replacing them with a more modern design can make a surprising difference.

Now you're ready to dress the room, neatly positioning a few well-chosen accessories. Fresh, fluffy towels are a luxurious must, as are new bars of scented soap. Pot-pourri and scented candles can help add a suggestion of other, more sensuous possibilities. If you replace your plant, make sure the new one is green and thriving. And last but not least, leave the loo seat firmly down – apart from anything else, in Feng Shui terms this will prevent you losing wealth. And, after all, that's what all this is about.

TOP 10 TIPS
FOR THE **BATHROOM**

1 No bathroom can be too clean, so use all your elbow grease to get surfaces really fresh and sparkling.

2 Declutter all surfaces. It's not necessary – or interesting – to have all your most intimate requirements on display.

3 Get rid of fitted carpets. They absorb moisture, often look tatty and smell bad.

4 Use only water resistant floor coverings here – lino, marmoleum, vinyl, ceramic or mosaic tiles.

5 If the tiles round the bath and basin are showing their age, apply a coat of specialist tile paint to bring them up to the minute.

6 Pot-pourri, scented candles, and pretty fragrant soaps and oils add something sensual to the atmosphere.

7 Ensure your privacy with a new blind on the window, or install frosted glass or plastic film for that frosted 'effect'.

8 Finish off all DIY jobs, install additional lighting and storage, if necessary.

9 Purchase a new shower curtain, toilet seat, and fresh, coordinating towels.

10 Badly stained or soiled grout should be cleaned or recoloured.

BATHROOM 1 BEFORE & AFTER

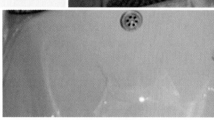

Use every ounce of elbow grease you can muster. Every surface of the room must be gleaming.

Replace old towels, flannels and bathmats with neatly folded, fluffy new ones.

Get rid of all inessential items. No buyer wants to know the intimate details of your ablutions.

DIAGNOSIS

Blocking the door to any room is bad Feng Shui and less than inviting. While the clutter here was bad enough, combined with the flower patterns on the wall, the atmosphere was frantic. Bathrooms should be spotlessly clean and tidy, and should enable buyers to imagine themselves luxuriating there. In this room there was far too much of the owner's personality present. It needed lightening up and decluttering to realise its potential.

DOCTOR'S ORDERS

With the paper stripped off and the walls painted a pastel green, the room seemed to be about three feet wider. I chose the colour because it went with the existing tiles and it is appropriately aquamarine. The carpet was a long way past its best so I replaced it with lino, which is hardwearing, waterproof and easy to clean (Top Tip 3).

Most important was to empty the room of the clutter, which was making it so crowded (Top Tip 2). When staging a bathroom, you need to put away every inessential item, leaving the room to speak for itself. There were plenty of shelves that the owner hadn't been able to resist filling and so I had to do a heavy editing job. Don't be tempted to pile your bath tidy with damp flannels and old bits of cracked soap. While you're selling your house, your bathroom must look as attractive as possible. We also moved the unnecessary furniture out, which meant that the door opened freely.

We cleaned every surface until it gleamed and sparkled, not forgetting round the back of the toilet (Top Tip 1). Privacy is obviously required so we invested in a new fabric blind for the window (Top Tip 7). A few finishing touches so often make all the difference to a bathroom. Brand-new towels, fresh scented soap and an arrangement of fresh flowers all helped in dressing it up (Top Tip 6).

DIAGNOSIS

My shriek could have been heard miles away. What on earth was a pet rat doing in the bathroom? Not only does it give the impression that the room's unhygienic, the smell of the creature and the sawdust get everywhere. Once I'd got over that, my attention turned to the rest of the room, with its extremely dated-looking fittings. The combination of floral tiles and wallpaper had a horribly dizzying effect, bringing the walls in and making the room seem very claustrophobic. Certainly, the carpet wasn't something you'd like to step onto after a bath. The whole room needed a really thorough clean and tidy, especially the dark fittings which show up watermarks and limescale. A window ledge was covered with unnecessary bits and pieces, while the window itself needed dressing. This was a case of having to improve the setting so the buyer's attention didn't dwell on the bathroom suite.

BATHROOM 2 BEFORE & AFTER

DOCTOR'S ORDERS

Obviously the first thing to go was the rat, swiftly followed by the carpet. Rather than replace a dark, old-fashioned suite, I chose to reduce its effect by improving things around it. We painted the wallpaper a warm apricot, which toned with the tiles and calmed the room down. Instead of the carpet, I chose a wood flooring in French rustic oak which, like the paint, contributed towards a much lighter effect (Top Tip 3).

Next, it was on with the rubber gloves for a really good clean, remembering every surface, from the skirting boards to the tiles (Top Tip 1). We put away all the cleaning products and personal belongings, none of which would appeal to a buyer wanting to imagine themselves using the room (Top Tip 2).

I wanted to break up the large expanse of wall above the tiling and chose a mirror to increase the amount of light in the room. The window wasn't a particularly attractive feature, so we bought a simple Roman blind which hid it, while still admitting as much light as possible (Top Tip 7). When we'd finished, the room definitely looked more inviting and much brighter than before.

Keep all pets out of the bathroom in the interests of hygiene.

Hide a nondescript window with a fine blind which doesn't block too much light.

Plain colours are calming and more restorative in a bathroom.

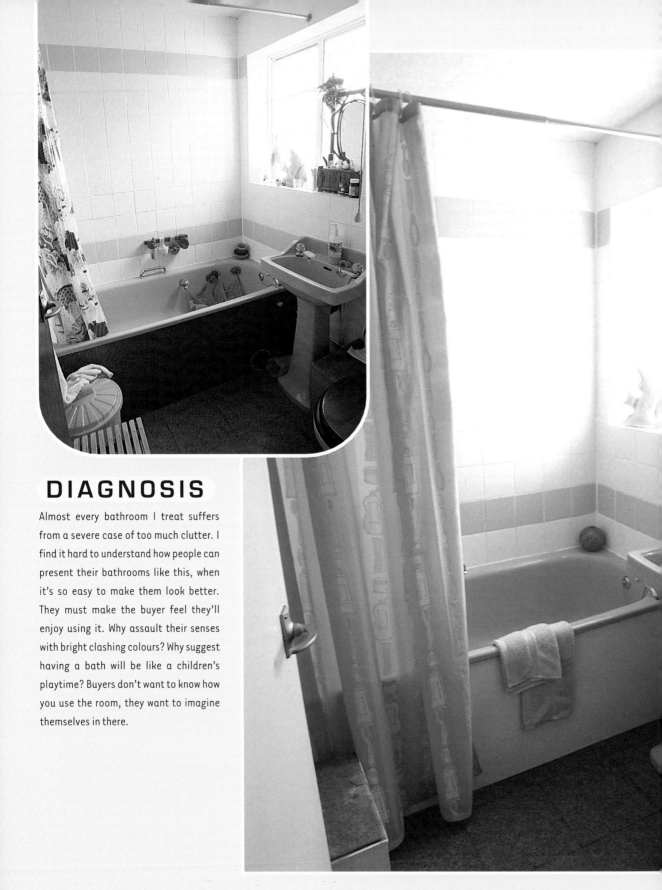

DIAGNOSIS

Almost every bathroom I treat suffers from a severe case of too much clutter. I find it hard to understand how people can present their bathrooms like this, when it's so easy to make them look better. They must make the buyer feel they'll enjoy using it. Why assault their senses with bright clashing colours? Why suggest having a bath will be like a children's playtime? Buyers don't want to know how you use the room, they want to imagine themselves in there.

BATHROOM 3
BEFORE & AFTER

DOCTOR'S ORDERS

The children's bathtime may be very precious, but not many buyers' hearts will be lifted by the sight of brightly coloured plastic toys littering what might one day be their bathroom. Besides, it takes their attention away from any good points the room may have (Top Tip 2).

Without the toys, we could concentrate on cleaning, as important as always, and tidying. In this bathroom the window sill was home to a jumble of things that hardly contributed to a soothing, restful atmosphere. I felt it was enough just to have the fish and the plant. Simple, but effective. A new blind added to the generally more sophisticated atmosphere I was aiming at. We chose a fine fabric that let light into the room but made it feel a more enclosed and personal space (Top Tip 7).

A new shower curtain is an inexpensive but effective way of changing the image of a bathroom (Top Tip 9). In this case the bright fishes were replaced by a more subtle and inoffensive blue curtain, which blended in with the colour scheme in the rest of the room. I'm always saying how important towels are when staging a bathroom and yet again, with the replacement of the used white one with neatly folded blue ones, the look was complete. We had changed the play area into a chic and comfortable bathroom to be appreciated by anyone.

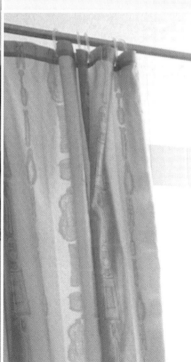

A new shower curtain which blends harmoniously with the rest of the fittings can give a whole new look to a bathroom.

Put away all children's toys while your house is on sale. Only get them out when needed.

Keep everything clean and simple to achieve the most striking and desirable effect.

CASE STUDY CAMDEN

A three-storey, three-bedroom Victorian house in London's Camden Town should have been snapped up. Kaz Brine's home had a price tag that suggested it was something pretty special but mysteriously, it had been on the market for three months with no takers.

Kaz Brine and her eighteen-year-old son, Zak, wanted to move from their house in London's trendy Camden Town, where they were a stone's throw from the busy market and the peace of Regent's Park. Properties in the area usually get snapped up for prices anywhere between £280,000 and £1 million.

The house itself certainly wasn't on the critical list, but buyers have the right to be picky if the price is high. I felt that we needed to lighten the place up and define the spaces better, particularly the living and dining areas. The two areas with huge unrealised potential were the master bedroom and the unfinished roof garden.

The outside led me to expect splendour within. However, I was met by a crowded hall painted in a deep red. The flamboyant colours I found here and in the living room were swiftly replaced to create an atmosphere of elegance and style. The red master bedroom, which looked as if a mass murder had been committed there, got the same treatment. Downstairs it was a question of moving Kaz's furniture around to best effect and removing the ostentatious TV from the wall. The living room led into an odd sitting area that resembled a waiting room with a view of a blank wall. This was much better utilised as a dining area. With the sofa removed, the radiator boxed in and a couple of candlesticks arranged on top and a picture above, things already looked better. We took the broken marble table top from the table on the roof, cut a piece of MDF, painted it black, then gold sized it before I showed Kaz how to apply green gold leaf. Hey presto, a sophisticated table for the new dining area. Our one real expense was the custom-made blinds in the living room, but windows like that deserve nothing less.

An indifferent seating area found better use as a sophisticated dining space in keeping with the rest of the house.

On the way upstairs we repaired the banisters. No point inviting a law suit when your buyer breaks his neck! Draping the curtains differently, I made a feature of the bay windows in the bedroom, which are the first thing you notice on entering the room. The cupboards and curtains were already blue and so, with the new wall colour, all I had to do was pull the room together with some new, coordinating bedlinen.

Finally, to the roof, where it was just a question of buying beautiful plants and bringing up the kitchen table and chairs which released the space downstairs. We simply created another room outside, immediately adding to the value of the house. Kaz was delighted with what we had done and even more pleased to receive an offer the day after we left.

An exotic oriental screen broke up a solid expanse of wall and lent an appropriate note of opulence to an otherwise undistinguished corner of the living room.

CASE STUDY CHELTENHAM

Jacqui and Mark Whitehead wanted to downsize the home they shared with their two children, Tom and Katy. They hoped to release some equity from the sale of their house and were anxious to know why it had been on the market for almost two months.

Cheltenham is a town with a Regency heritage, famous for its gardens and racecourse. The housing market was at a premium when we visited, with houses selling within a week of being put up for sale. However, the Whiteheads' three-bedroom house hadn't budged after almost two months.

I had to be rather harsher on the Whiteheads than on many clients. They were living in denial, surrounded by chaos. Most buyers can't see beyond the clutter and simply think: 'They live like this. I can't'. The hall was bright but there were so many swirls in the glass door, the wallcovering and the carpet, it was enough to drive anyone crazy. After replacing the glass, repainting, recarpeting and tidying, I moved into the dining room. I loved the shade of red on the wall but everywhere else took eclecticism to new heights with Japanese screens, Indian cushions and Mexican tiles. The Whiteheads hadn't defined

the purpose of the room or settled on a style. We reinstated the hatch that led into the kitchen and then made it into a multi-functional room where the children, Tom and Katy, could do homework or watch TV, or the whole family could sit down for meals and chat together.

The first thing I saw on walking into the living room was the old Christmas tree hidden behind the sofa. But that was just the beginning. In a bored moment, Jacqui had decorated the walls in an orange sponge effect. The tree was found a new home (in the dump) while the walls were repainted a more sophisticated neutral shade that was easier on the eye. I discovered some great antique furniture in the basement, which looked terrific here. To make a screen to hide the TV, I hinged together the frames for a flat-pack shelving unit, then covered it with fabric, which added a splash of colour to the room.

The Mexican tiles round the dining room fireplace stood out when the clutter in the rest of the room was edited and defined.

Upstairs was far worse. The master bedroom had been given over to Tom. It was a nightmare that would put anybody off the house. Despite protests, I moved Tom out into the second bedroom and then stripped the posters from the wall before reinstating it as an elegant and calming master bedroom. Mark and Jacqui had been using the second bedroom and when I saw it, I could see exactly where Tom had got his ideas from. The room was ruthlessly tidied, the bed was made with fresh linen and the radiator boxed in as a bench unit.

Mark and Jacqui had wrongly assumed that buyers could see through their mess to the house beneath. Together we thoroughly cleared it and presented their home in a way that suited its period and size. The day I left, the Whiteheads received an offer at the full asking price.

Little needed to be done in the kitchen apart from completing unfinished jobs. The walls were painted in yellow to tone with the tiles and to bring in contrasting blue accents.

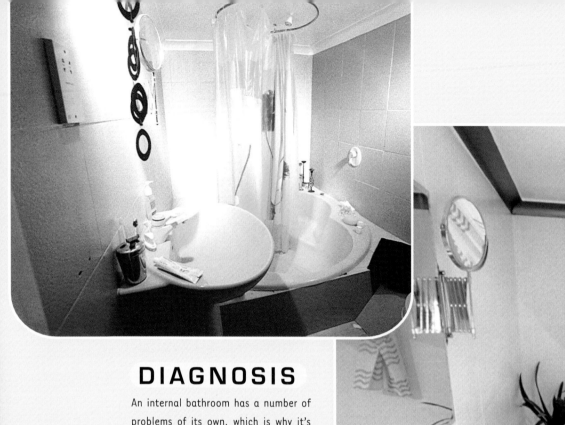

DIAGNOSIS

An internal bathroom has a number of problems of its own, which is why it's doubly important to stage it properly. The most obvious difficulties are lack of natural light and poor ventilation. This bathroom had additional problems because it was so small and the owner had done his best to make it seem even smaller with those dreary green walls, the ugly hanging plastic curtain and mobile. The finishing touches of a half-squeezed toothpaste tube, some shaving kit and other personal effects just didn't cut it at all. Most buyers would only want to spend the shortest possible time in there, which was not going to get the house sold. To turn this bathroom into a selling point rather than a minus point, I had to create the impression of space and style.

BATHROOM 4 BEFORE & AFTER

DOCTOR'S ORDERS

If the room was to look any bigger, the tiles had to be painted. Special tile paint is available from most DIY stores and swiftly smooths over any glaring horrors in the bathroom or kitchen (Top Tip 5). In this case I chose white, simply because it would give the most impression of space. We painted the coving a subtle grey to give a sense of enclosure. The other obvious trick to gain space was to hang a mirror over the basin.

A new shower curtain tied in with the sophisticated new colour scheme, but I tied it back for when it would be out of use (Top Tip 9). Another way to make the room seem a lot larger.

Once we'd got rid of all the clutter from the surfaces (Top Tip 1), everything could be cleaned relentlessly before we added the finishing touches. Scented soap and pot-pourri appealed to the senses, while the plant lent a feeling of movement and colour, too (Top Tip 6). I had a new towel rail fitted and bought grey towels to tie the look together (Top Tip 9). With a little imagination and care, the room looked loved and inviting.

Special tile paint can be used to hide a multitude of sins.

Avoid heavy colours that could make the space seem smaller than it really is.

Tying a shower curtain back provides a greater sense of space here.

DIAGNOSIS

This bathroom badly needed rescuing
from a time-warp. The original wallpaper,
no doubt fashionable when it was put up
twenty years earlier, looked hopelessly
out of date, while the carpet covered
even the side of the bath. I couldn't do
anything about the yellow fittings, but I
could minimise their impact by changing
what was round them. Clutter, dried
flowers — it all had to go. Somehow I
had to drag this bathroom kicking and
screaming into the new millennium.

BATHROOM 5 BEFORE & AFTER

DOCTOR'S ORDERS

I've only ever seen carpet on the sides of English baths and it always strikes me as a bad idea. It can only get damp, tired and smelly, though perhaps not quite as badly as carpet on the floor. In this instance I chose to replace it with self-adhesive floor tiles to give a much slicker finish to the room (Top Tip 3).

The wallpaper was obliterated by painting over it in a shade that complemented the bathroom suite. A dated-looking wooden window frame was swiftly glossed over in white. I refused to allow back any of the clutter that had accumulated. The pictures that weren't even hung straight were replaced by one print, which hung in place of the overcrowded and redundant shelving unit. And the window sill looked much better, too, with a neat set of bath products and a plant.

I don't like to see dried flowers anywhere in the house but least of all in the bathroom. What's wrong with the real thing? Yes, they eventually die, but until then they look good, can smell wonderful and don't gather dust. Nothing looks worse than untended plants. If you use potted ones, make sure that you remove any dead leaves and polish those that remain. Clean, carefully folded towels and a fresh bar of soap were the only other accessories needed to kickstart this bathroom into the twenty-first century (Top Tips 6 & 9).

One tip: I should have left the toilet seat down. It looks so much better and in Feng Shui terms you risk flushing energy and money away.

The most old-fashioned bathroom can be improved with new flooring and a lick of paint, too.

Plants must be well-tended if they are to add anything to a room.

Adhesive floor tiles are easy to lay and can give a light, modern effect.

OUTSIDE

sold

Has your house got kerb appeal? If it hasn't and you want a quick sale, it's time to address the problems. Buyers must be made to want to come into your house and not drive straight past it. A messy exterior throws up a red flag to them. After all, if you don't pay attention to the outside of the house, what's the inside going to be like?

Tidy up the garden (front and back), removing all signs of children, pets and rubbish. If necessary, define the boundaries of the house with the addition of fencing. Prune trees if you can. They look better and will let more light into the house. Make sure the windows are clean and curtains are straight.

No matter how small your garden may be, you must make the most of it. It represents cash in your pocket – it's as simple as that. Providing an extra outdoor room will add value to your house. You may have been meaning to clear the jungle for months. Now's the time to do it. Tidy up existing plants and brighten things up with some border plants from the garden centre. If necessary, lay new turf – your buyer wants a garden, not a football pitch.

Invest in some garden furniture and make an area where it will be pleasant to sit out and entertain. If the garden is troubled by traffic noise, then a small water feature will help disguise it and introduces a welcoming sense of calm, too.

If you live in the city and have access to a roof terrace, it is just as important to turn it into a haven away from the chaos of urban life. Make sure the area is kept clean and tidy. You need pot plants (bought or hired) to create the right atmosphere here. A small outdoor table and chairs are essential.

Always remember that, when in the garden, your buyer will notice the back of the house, so carry out the same checks as you did for the front. Painting the back door and standing a potted plant beside it will make it look cheerful and welcoming.

That's it. Your house is now ready for that quick sale. Good luck.

TOP 10 TIPS FOR OUTSIDE

1 Define your boundaries. Buyers need to know exactly what they are getting for their money, so if necessary, invest in some new fencing.

2 Mow the grass, weed the flowerbeds and purchase some flowering border plants to give life and colour to the dingiest garden.

3 Make sure you have adequate lighting, in front and at the back of your home.

4 Don't forget about how your house looks when viewed from the garden – paint exterior walls a bright welcoming colour.

5 Turf over your children's football pitch and keep them off it until the house is sold.

6 Make an area where you can put a garden table and chairs. Immediately it transforms a garden or conservatory into another area that can be enjoyed in the sun.

7 Paint your front and back doors and polish all the door furniture so it gleams. It immediately suggests you take as much care of the inside. Be sure that your house numbers are easily visible.

8 Put a container or two of flowers, or a hanging basket, as a welcome by the front and back door.

9 Add an interesting water feature, an attractive garden light, or even some garden sculpture as a finishing touch.

10 Have a regular weekly maintenance programme to keep the outside of your home looking great throughout the whole marketing period.

OUTSIDE 1 BEFORE & AFTER

Make a bold and colourful statement with a brightly painted fence and lush hanging baskets.

Clearing away all the winter detritus makes a roof terrace appear loved and looked after.

DIAGNOSIS

More a plant cemetery than a roof garden, this outdoor space needed urgent treatment. Space like this is at a premium in a busy city and it's madness not to make the most of it. Having gone to all the trouble of having the terrace designed, the owner had completely lost heart during the bad weather and failed to finish it off.

A cracked marble table, a few miserable straggling plants and a naked gazebo did not make an earthly paradise.

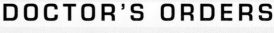

DOCTOR'S ORDERS

This was the only outdoor space belonging to the house so it was important to make the most of it. Although it was winter, the first port of call was the garden centre, where we chose a number of plants, some for colour and some for presence (Top Tip 2). I particularly liked the bamboos, which are delicate, whisper in the wind and grow quickly. The pots were already on the terrace so it was just a question of filling them with the most appropriate things until it began to look more like a garden space.

I had plans to use the table inside the house. However, the cracked top lent easily against the terrace wall to disguise some pipes. Instead, we brought up a round table, which I felt went better with the space, its curves echoing those of the gazebo and providing a contrast with the angular shapes of the terrace itself.

Otherwise all that was required was a good sweep to make the place look loved and cared for and a slight rearrangement of the furniture and statuary. It's attending to such small details as these that adds pounds to the sale of your house.

Even in winter, flowering plants can be bought to cheer up a neglected outdoor space.

DIAGNOSIS

I sometimes have to remind clients that although they're working hard to stage the inside of their house, they must pay attention to the outside, too.

In this case, the pebble dash was painted an extremely off-putting pink, which I felt was a large strike against this property. Viewers would approach the house with a negative attitude before they'd even set foot inside it.

At the rear of the house there was a large paved area and this was apparently unused. It was scruffy and uninviting – a shame when it should be presented as a positive bonus, being another room to the house.

The exterior of this house immediately cried out 'old-fashioned and neglected'. These were the issues I had to address.

OUTSIDE 2 BEFORE & AFTER

DOCTOR'S ORDERS

I don't believe you can underestimate the importance of kerb appeal. Any potential buyer must be made to approach your house in the most positive frame of mind. I decided to blow a large part of the budget on repainting the exterior of this house, changing the ugly pink to a sophisticated cream. And it worked. The house looked larger, more elegant and as if the owners still cared for it. It immediately suggests that the same will be true of the inside.

Any outdoor space is a bonus and must be presented as such. It's no good expecting buyers to imagine how your garden might be transformed into a place for entertaining and enjoyment. You have to do the work for them. This patio was the ideal space for sitting out and enjoying the sun. All it took was the addition of a garden table and chairs and it was obvious what pleasures this garden had in store (Top Tip 6). The addition of some flowering plants cheered things up no end (Top Tip 2). When doing up your garden, remember to look back at the house to make sure that you like what you can see, both outside and inside.

Pebble-dashed or rendered exteriors often benefit from being repainted.

Turn an empty patio into another room with the addition of a set of garden furniture.

Dead, unattended plants must be replaced with strong healthy ones.

CASE STUDY PORTISHEAD

Dave Kather and Jessica Westley lived with their baby son Eli in a bungalow overlooking the Gordano Valley. They were mystified as to why their home had been on the estate agents' books for over four months.

Portishead is a sleepy seaside town overlooking the Severn Bridge and fifteen minutes away from Bristol. Dave Kather and Jessica Westley's house was on a beautiful site in the town but it was immediately obvious that they had simply accumulated far too much inside and were successfully hiding its potential.

Outside there was a severe lack of kerb appeal. The grass was uncared for, the chipped and cracked pots containing some dead or straggly plants. All that was easily remedied. However, inside it was more tricky. The hall was the worst entrance I've ever seen and typified the rest of the house. It was untidy, unfinished and painted a wild shade of orange with purple shelves. It's all very well to live with a wacky range of vibrant colours but it's not a cocktail that your buyer will necessarily fall for. Buyers tend to make their minds up within three minutes of walking into the house and if they immediately have a negative,

subliminal reaction, they won't buy and they won't even know why. In the hall we cleared away the clutter of a lifetime, removed the door-height bookshelves and painted it all an off-white with white doors to double the space. The storage heater was boxed in, making a shelf which I used to create a vignette.

The dining room was multi-functional mayhem. First, came a major clear-out (including the old fireplace), a lick or two of paint and the fitting of a new carpet. Usually, I like to rearrange what's already in the house, but this time little was reusable. Dave and Jessica agreed to buy a new dining table and chairs, bookcase and home office unit which would all go with them to their new home. The finishing touch was the addition of coving round the ceiling. Their sitting room had become a padded cell for Eli, who bounced from one sofa lined up against the wall to another. We therefore released the space by getting rid of all the

The dark cork tiles were removed from one wall and the walls repainted. Then we added the masterstroke – a breakfast bar.

furniture, revealing the original floorboards, moving the piano in from the dining room and buying one pristine sofa. The green-and-white colour scheme gave the room a feeling of togetherness and space it didn't have before. Although the kitchen left a bit to be desired, there wasn't a lot we could do except declutter and clean it thoroughly. I know cats have to eat, but they don't have to eat all day. Any kitchen looks better without animal bowls.

The bedroom was tidied, painted and coordinated with new curtains and bedlinen. Most important was the plastering of their peeled ceiling, which could have put suspicious buyers off.

When I left, Dave and Jessica were quite confident that the house, although not necessarily decorated to their taste any more, would soon sell. And sure enough, the next day they received an offer which they accepted.

Tidying the unbelievable clutter from every surface and painting the wooden wardrobes with white gloss gave the bedroom a new lease of life. Flowers completed the look.

SELLING YOUR HOME

WHY USE AN ESTATE AGENT?

Although your house is ready to sell, you are not out of the woods yet — it's time to find an estate agent. The right agent can make the difference between your house selling quickly at the right price or languishing on the market forever. While the agent must be a good salesperson, he or she also needs a basic grounding in finance, law, building and, occasionally, even interior design — and should have the relevant experts at his or her fingertips when necessary.

HOW TO CHOOSE AN AGENT

There are so many estate agents it's hard to know which one to pick. So to find one you can trust and rely on, it's worth spending a little time doing your research first.

- **Choose a specialist** It's important to select an agent who specialises in your area if your house is to be valued at its correct price and given high local visibility. Also, the agent needs to be knowledgeable enough to answer any questions a potential buyer may have about the surrounding area.

- **Keep in touch** Let the agent know you're serious about making a quick sale.

- **Avoid using friends or family** However good an agent a friend may be, if something goes wrong your relationship may not stand the strain. If someone you know can recommend an agent based on experience, so much the better.

- **Choose someone you can trust** Look for an agent who meets your particular needs as they will be representing you to the buying public. Selling a house is an emotional event. You need to feel your agent is someone to whom you can always relate.

- **Be selective** Take time to interview at least three agencies and ask them exactly how they are going to market your home and, of course, how they value it.

- **Do your research** Ask if you can contact previous clients for references and to see a list detailing the sales that they've achieved in the previous eighteen months.

- **Protect yourself** Only employ an agent who is a member of the National Association of Estate Agents in order to protect yourself if a problem arises later on.

- **Don't skimp** Remember that you usually get what you pay for. Don't automatically choose the agent charging the lowest commission.

- **Hedge your bets** For greater exposure, you may want to use more than one agent, but always remember that quantity probably won't produce quality of service.

- **Expect the best** Make it clear from the very outset exactly what you expect of your agent. This way, you run little danger of being let down.

- **Work together** Finally, having chosen your agent, co-operate as best you can and try to avoid any misunderstandings. After all, you're both working towards one goal: the swift and successful sale of your home.

WHAT TO LOOK FOR IN YOUR NEW HOME

AND WHAT YOUR BUYER MAY LOOK FOR IN YOURS

Staging your home for sale is only one part of the equation. If you're selling, you're most likely to be buying a new home too, so I think it's worth providing a few pointers to help you to be sure that it's the right one for you, as well as reminding you how buyers may be researching your home.

- **Is it for you?** Mentally strip the house of its furniture and look at the space itself, imagining how it will suit your kind of lifestyle and possessions. If you have trouble envisaging that, get a friend or a professional to help.

- **Structure** Look for any red flags that might suggest something more sinister is wrong with the house. Check for signs of damp, cracks, mould, subsidence – anything unusual that catches your eye. The excessive use of air fresheners might be covering something unwelcome.

- **Fittings** Look at the floors and windows, and ensure they don't need replacing.

- **Major repairs** Ascertain whether you will have to refit the bathroom or the kitchen, that the wiring is sound and that the central heating system works properly. All these things are expensive to replace and you will not want those unexpected costs when you move in.

- **Space** Check there's space for any particular fittings or appliances you may have.

- **Storage** Ensure there will be room for your larger items of furniture and enough storage and cupboard space.

- **Hidden extras** Look underneath carpets to see the flooring beneath. If one day you're looking forward to having stripped floorboards, you will be disappointed later to discover that the floors are in fact concrete slab.

- **Ask the experts** Get a professional in to check the structure of the house and have a lawyer go carefully through the deeds, conduct a local authority search and administrate your acquisition. You could do it yourself but it's a lengthy and detailed procedure best left to someone with experience.

- **Take a second look** Visit the property at different times of the day to see if it is affected by traffic, local noise or fumes. You can also see where the sun falls on the property and at which time of day.

- **Check the boundaries** Ensure the boundaries of the property are exactly those described in the particulars (your lawyer should be able to help you with this).

- **Get to know the area** Sound out the facilities that may be relevant to you – schools, amenities, plans for future development – to avoid unpleasant surprises.

- **Talk to the neighbours** Get a real sense of the neighbourhood, then weigh up the positive aspects against the negative ones.

- **On the up?** Find out whether the area is on the up or has peaked. If you're not planning on living there for long, this is an important consideration.

- **Why is it for sale?** Find out why the owners are selling. The chances are if they can't live with the barking dog or the loud music, you won't be able to either.

- **Is the price right?** Check what sort of price other properties have sold for in the area, so that you can gauge whether or not your price is right.

- But most importantly of all, whatever the particular circumstances or idiosyncrasies of the property you are buying, **it must feel like home**.

RESOURCES

GENERAL

ADS Recycling
63 Camsley Lane
Lymm
Warrington
Cheshire WA13 9BY
Tel: 01925 757 033
www.recycling.co.uk

ARC (fine art publishers)
1–6 Andrew Place
Cowthorpe Road
London SW8 4RA
Tel: 020 7731 3933
www.arcprints.com

B&Q
Portswood House
1 Hampshire Corporate Park
Chandlers Ford
Hampshire SO53 3YX
Head office: 023 8025 6256
Store location: 020 7576 6502
www.diy.com

Cargo Homeshops
Thame Park Industrial Estate
Domer Road
Thame
Oxfordshire
OX9 3HD
Tel: 01844 261800

Cornelissen & Son Ltd (fine art supplies)
105 Great Russell Street
London WC1B 3RY
Tel: 020 7636 1045
Fax: 020 7636 3655
Info@cornelissen.com

Focus Do It All
Gaws Worth House
Westmere Drive
Crewe
Cheshire
CW1 6XB
Tel: 0800 436 436
www.Focusdoitall.co.uk

Hanley & Woods (furniture manufacturer)
16 Chetham Court
Winwick Quay
Warrington
Cheshire WA2 8RF
Tel: 01925 634 941

Habitat
196 Tottenham Court Road
London W1T 9LG
For stockists: 0845 980 1800
www.habitat.net

Heals
196 Tottenham Court Road
London W1T 7LQ
Tel: 020 7636 1666
www.heals.co.uk

Homebase
Beddington House
Railway Approach
Wallington, Surrey SM6 0HB
Tel: 0845980 1800
www.homebase.co.uk

Laura Ashley
Home Customer Services
PO Box 19
Newtown
Powys SY16 1DZ
Tel: 01686 22333
www.lauraashley.com

Marks & Spencer
Michael House
47-67 Baker Street
London W1V 8EP
Tel: 020 7935 4422
www.marks-and-spencer.co.uk

Millennium Interiors
23 London Road
Stockton Heath Village
South Warrington
Cheshire WA4 6SG
Tel: 01925 210010
www.millenium-interiors.co.uk

Next
Desford Road
Enderby
Leicestershire LE9 5AT
Tel (stockists): 08702 435 435
www.next.co.uk

Ocean Home Shopping
689 Mitcham Road
Croydon CR0 3AF
Tel: 0870 2426283
www.oceancatalogue.com

The Pier
200 Tottenham Court Road
London W1P 0AD
Tel: 020 7637 7001
Tel (mail order): 020 7814 5004
Fax: 020 7637 3332
www.pier.co.uk

Wickes (head office) (DIY store)
120-138 Station Road
Harrow
Middlesex HA1 2QB
Customer enquiries tel: 0500 300328
www.wickes.co.uk

IKEA
255 North Circular Road
London
NW10 0JQ
Tel: 020 8208 5600
www.ikea.co.uk

Inspiration
52-56 Frodsham Street
Chester
CH1 3LB
Tel: 01244 313703

John Lewis
Oxford Street
London
W1A 1EX
Tel: 020 7629 7711
www.johnlewis.co.uk

Kays Catalogue
Kay & Co
Marshall Street
Leeds LS11 9YX
Tel orders: 0845 952 9529
www.kay.com

ACCESSORIES

Christy Towels
PO Box 19
Newton Street
Hyde
Cheshire SK14 4NR
Tel: 0161 3681961
www.christy-towels.com

Elephant
230 Tottenham Court Road
London W1P 9AE
Tel: 020 7637 7930

J Kenney (curtain service)
489 Hackney Road
London E2 9ED
Tel: 020 7729 2766

CARPETS & FLOORING

The Alternative Flooring Company
3B Stephenson Close
East Portway
Andover
Hampshire
SP10 3RU
Stockists: 01264 335111
www.alternative-flooring.co.uk

Carpetwise
Unit 5
St Catherine's Retail Park
St Catherine's Road
Perth PH1 5XA
Tel: 01738 621 641

Central Flooring Sanding
131 Drumbrae Drive
Edinburgh EH4 7SL
Tel: 0131 653 3111

Kingsmead Carpets
Caponacre Industrial Estate
Cumnock
Ayrshire DA18 1SH
Tel: 01290 421511
www.kingsmead.carpet.info.com

Natural Flooring Direct
46 Webbs Road
London SW11 6SF
Tel: 0800 454721
e-mail: nfd@eidonet.co.uk

Pentonville Rubber
104–106 Pentonville Road
London N1 9JB
Tel: 020 7837 4582

Tomkinsons Carpets Limited
PO Box 11, Duke Place
Kidderminster
Worcestershire DY10 2JR
Tel: 01562 820006
e-mail: Floors@tomkinsons.co.uk

FABRICS

B Brown Display Fabrics
74–78 Wood Lane End
Hemel Hempstead
Hertfordshire HP2 4RF
Tel: 08705 340 340
www.bbrown.co.uk

Cotswold Fabric Warehouse
5 Tewkesbury Road
Cheltenham GL51 9AH
Tel: 01242 255959

The Curtain Mill
46–52 Fairfield Road
London E3 2QB
Tel: 020 8980 9000
Fax: 020 8981 7977

Dunelm Mills
3-6 The Rushes
Loughborough
Leicestershire LE11 0BE
Tel: 01509 234717
www.dunelm-mills.co.uk

Ponder Mills Linens
8 Paddock Row
Grosvenor Precinct
Chester CH1 1ED
Tel: 01244 340537

FIREPLACES
Marble Hill Fireplaces
70-72 Richmond Road
Twickenham
Middlesex TW1 3BE
Tel: 020 8892 1488
www.marblehill.co.uk

LIGHTING
Christopher Wray
591-593 King's Road
London SW6 2YW
Catalogue tel: 020 7384 2888
Enquiries tel: 020 7736 8434
www.christopher-wray.com

PAINTS & WALLCOVERINGS
Anaglypta
Akzo Nobel Decorative Coatings Ltd
PO Box 37
Crown House
Hollins Road
Darwen
Lancashire BB3 0BG
Tel: 01254 870 137
www.anaglypta.co.uk

Crown Paints
Akzo Nobel Decorative Coatings Ltd
PO Box 37
Crown House
Hollins Road
Darwen
Lancashire BB3 0BG
Tel (stockists): 01254 704951
Fax: 01254 704212
www.crownpaint.co.uk

Dulux Paints
ICI Paint
Wexham Road
Slough
Berkshire SL2 5DS
Tel: 01753 550000
Advice tel line (retail): 01753 556998
Advice tel line (trade): 01753 559991
www.dulux.co.uk

Sandtex
Akzo Nobel Decorative Coatings Ltd
PO Box 37
Crown House
Hollins Road
Darwen
Lancashire BB3 0BG
Tel (stockists): 01254 704951
Fax: 01254 704212
www.sandtex.co.uk

OUTSIDE
Camden Garden Centre
2 Barker Drive
St Pancras Way
London NW1 0JW
Tel: 020 7485 8468
www.hart-ltd.co.uk

Cantilever Garden Centre
Station Road
Latchford
Warrington
Cheshire WA4 2AB
Tel: 01925 635799
e-mail: ktilling@tcofcheshire.unet.com

Warrington Fencing Manufacturers
New Cut Lane Industrial Estate
Woolston
Warrington
Cheshire WA1 6UD
Tel: 01925 823227

TILING
Ceramic Prints Ltd
George Street
Armitage Road Industrial Estate
Brighouse
West Yorkshire HD6 1PU
Tel: 01484 712522

Worlds End Tiles
Silverthorne Road
Battersea
London SW8 3HE
Tel: 020 7819 2100
www.worldsendtiles.co.uk

OTHER
The Property Trade Directory
5th Floor, 29-30 Warwick Street
London W1R 5RD
Tel: 020 8800 2262
Fax: 020 8800 2021